Angels Defiant

Angels Defiant

Two Accounts of Pilots on the Western Front
During the First World War 1914-1918

Above the French Lines
Stuart Walcott

The American Spirit
Briggs Kilburn Adams

LEONAUR

Angels Defiant
Two Accounts of Pilots on the Western Front During the First World War 1914-1918
Above the French Lines
by Stuart Walcott
and
The American Spirit
by Briggs Kilburn Adams

First published under the titles
Above the French Lines
and
The American Spirit

FIRST EDITION

Leonaur is an imprint
of Oakpast Ltd

Copyright in this form © 2014 Oakpast Ltd

ISBN: 978-1-78282-293-6 (hardcover)
ISBN: 978-1-78282-294-3 (softcover)

http://www.leonaur.com

Contents

Above the French Lines

STUART WALCOTT IN HIS AEROPLANE

Contents

Benjamin Stuart Walcott

Introduction

(From the *Princeton Alumni Weekly* of January 30, 1918.)

It is now seven weeks since the dispatches from Paris reported that Stuart Walcott was attacked by three German airplanes and brought down behind the German lines, after he himself had brought down a German plane in his first combat on December 12, 1917, and that it was feared he had been killed; but even now, after the lapse of nearly two months, it is not definitely known whether his fall proved fatal, or whether the earnest hope of his friends that he is still alive may be realised. The reports are conflicting. A cable message of January 7 said that in Germany it was reported that S. Walcott had been killed by a fall on December 12 near Saint Souplet; but Dr. Walcott received a letter on January 19 which holds out some hope that the fall was not fatal and that his son may be a prisoner in Germany. This letter, dated December 17, is from a young aviator named Loughran,[1] who was Stuart Walcott's roommate at the flying station. He gives this report of what was told to him by an observer and pilot who saw the combat:

> On the 12th of December at 11:30 a. m., there were five pilots to go out on high patrol, including Stuart and myself. But I was prevented from going, because of a wrenched ankle. Stuart and the other pilots left here at 11:40 a. m. for high patrol, which means they are to fly above the thousand metres. Two of the pilots had to return because of motor trouble, leaving one pilot whom Stuart was following.
>
> At 12:50 a. m. they ran across a German bi-place machine. The French pilot attacked first, but had to withdraw because of

---

1. Loughran himself was killed in combat, in February, 1918. Attacked within the German lines, by four enemy planes, he succeeded in getting back over the French lines, but was there brought down. He was buried near Châlons. The Lafayette Escadrille attended his funeral.

trouble with his machine gun. He reports that the Spad (Stuart Walcott's machine), that had been following him, he last saw a thousand metres above him, or the German. Also that the German had gone back over his lines. The infantry and artillery observers report the French pilot's attack and combat. And that six minutes later the German returned over our lines. And that the Spad that was seen flying at a very high altitude, came down and attacked the German, and succeeded in bringing him down in flames. In doing so he had to fly quite a way over the German territory. And that the Spad had started to return, when three German fighting machines were seen diving on him, and forcing him down. The Spad was last seen doing a nose-dive perpendicular, behind their lines. That is all the information I have received up to date.

This is what makes all the boys think that Stuart is alive:

A nose-dive perpendicular is used very often in combat, but is very dangerous, as it is very difficult for one to come out of and yet have their motor running; that reason might force him to land; also there was very little chance for him to get away from them by flying, as they were above, and the only sensible thing to do was to land; and as we were only three days in this *secteur*, the French think he might have been mixed up as to the direction for home; or that he was slightly wounded and could not turn his machine toward the French lines.

I have tried every way possible to get information about Stuart. I have sent the numbers of his motor and machine to Major Sykes, who is trying to trace it through the Red Cross service.

One of the French pilots of this *escadrille*, who is a very good friend of your boy, shot down a German biplane on 18th of December. The machine fell behind our lines. The pilot was dead before reaching the ground. But the observer was only slightly wounded, so the boys of that *escadrille* have asked the commander of the group if we could be permitted to go and talk to the German, as he may know something about the Spad that fell behind his lines the day before. We hope to know whether we will be permitted to do so or not, tomorrow.

It takes two months before we receive the report from Germany officially. In the meantime you will read all sorts of reports in the newspapers. But I will cable or have Capt. Peter Boal do so, if I get any news that is true.

The case of Buckley, the American who fell Sept 5, was reported as being in flames from five thousand metres down, and fell in German territory. The observers reported that it landed on its back and burned completely. His parents were notified of his death; newspapers reported the terrible death he died. Well, Sir, on November 25 we received a letter from him, saying he was enjoying the best of health and was satisfied with his surroundings in the prison camp in Germany.

So we are all hoping the same for Stuart. I have all Stuart's personal things, and will give them to Capt. Boal the first chance I get.

Mr. Walcott, it is beyond words for me to try and tell you how grieved we all are about Stuart, and how great a loss it is to the *escadrille*. for him to be away. He was more than liked by every member and officer, and gave promise of doing great things, was always up in his machine trying to better himself in combat flying; there never was a minute that he was idle, if it was possible for him to fly. And never a more generous and kinder boy. Only the night before the patrol he last went out on, he gave me every care in the world, got up during the night to make sure I was comfortable and to do anything he could for my ankle.

From one who has been with Stuart through all his training, and room-mate on the Front,

Yours respectfully,

E. J. Loughran.

This letter was written before the cable dispatch of January 7, from the International Red Cross, which seems to establish definitely the fact that Stuart Walcott gave his life in support of the endeavour to "make the world safe for democracy." In further and final evidence, a letter dated February 5, 1918, informed Dr. Walcott that the Red Cross agent in Paris had reported "Stuart Walcott's grave has been found." An accompanying map from Loughran shows that the spot where Stuart Walcott fell is on a hill a little South of Saint Souplet.

★★★★★★

Benjamin Stuart Walcott was of New England ancestry. His earliest known American forbear was Capt. Jonathan Walcott of Salem, Mass., 1663-1699. Later, one of Capt. Jonathan's descendants, Benjamin Stuart Walcott, served in a Rhode Island regiment during the Revolutionary War. On his mother's side two ancestors served in the Continental Army and in the Revolutionary War.

Stuart Walcott was a senior at Princeton in the winter of 1916-17. In view of his approaching graduation in the spring his father wrote to him that he had best begin to think about what he was to do after graduation in order that he might get on an independent basis as soon as practicable. In response under date of January 7, 1917, he wrote:

You spoke of my being independent after I graduate in the spring. If I go to Europe, as I want to, to drive an ambulance or in the aeroplane I will be doing a man's work and shall be doing enough to support myself. If the work is unpaid, it is merely because it is charitable work and as such is given freely. If you want to pay my way, I will consider it not as dependence on you, father, but as a partnership that may help the Allies and their cause. I will furnish my services and you the funds to make my services available. If not, I will be willing to invest the small amount of capital which has accumulated in my name. I have been thinking of this work in Europe for over a year now, and am still very strong for it. I don't know what the effect will be on myself, but if it will be of service to others, I think that it is something I ought to do.

Being assured that the expenses would be provided for, he then began an investigation as to the best method of procedure to obtain training as an aviator. In a letter dated January 26 he said:

Many, many thanks for sending me the book on the French Flying Corps by Winslow. I read half of it the night that it came and stayed up late last night to finish it. He gives a very straight, interesting and apparently not exaggerated account of the work over there, which has made it somewhat clearer to me, just what it is that I want to get into. Now I am even more anxious than I was before to join the service over there. The more that I think about it and the more that I hear of it, the more desirous I am of getting into the Flying Corps. If a man like Winslow with a wife and daughter dependent on him is willing to take the risk involved, I see no reason why I should not.
You mention the Ambulance service in your last note. I have thought of that quite a little and would definitely prefer the aviation. The ambulance is worthwhile, I think, in that it gives one an opportunity to be of great service to humanity, but not so much so as the other. There will be a number of my class-mates who will enlist in the American Ambulance this spring,

but the air service appeals to me.

He then made arrangements with the American representatives of the Lafayette Escadrille to go to France on the completion of his college year. On January 29 he wrote:

I will get a physical examination in a few days. In regard to getting the training over here first, I do not think that it would be worth while. The instruction over there would be first hand, bright, for a definite purpose and on the whole superior to what I could get here. I could also be picking up the language and the hang of the country at the same time.

On February 24 he received word that his papers presented with his application for admittance to the Franco-American Flying Corps assured him on their face of a welcome when he presented himself in Paris. He was informed that if he utilized his spare time in availing himself of any and every opportunity to familiarize himself with flying, it would shorten his stay in the Student Aviators School in France. On March 26 he wrote:

I haven't been able to find out anything definite about the school at Mineola. As yet, no change has been announced to my knowledge, in reference to hastening up the course in event of the coming of war. Over a hundred men have left college [Princeton] already to start training for the Mosquito Fleet, and the rest of them are drilling every afternoon. What do you think of the advisability of stopping college and going to some aviation school? Considering that it takes several months to become at all useful as an aviator and that war is practically inevitable now, I think it would be wise to get started right away.

And again, on April 3:

I saw in the morning paper that the American fliers in Finance would be transferred to American registry immediately after the declaration of war. When you next see General Squier, I wish that you would sound him on the probability of a force being sent to France to learn to fly according to French methods. That is the one thing above all others that I want to get into. If there is any chance of that I do not want to get involved in anything else
It is quite certain that seniors who leave college now, to go into

military work, will receive their degrees. I would not object to losing the work as it is not my present intention to keep on with theoretical chemistry and that is what I am devoting my time to this spring. From the standpoint of education alone, I think that my time could be more profitably spent in the study of aviation.

Leave was granted by the University, and on April 6 Stuart Walcott was appointed a special assistant to Mr. Sidney D. Waldon, Inspector of Aeroplanes and Aeroplane Motors, Signal Service at Large. He immediately reported to Mr. Waldon and worked with him through April. May first he went to Newport News, Virginia. May 2 he reported:

My first trip up was this afternoon with Victor Carlstrom. We were out 16 minutes and climbed 3,500 feet. It was all very simple getting up there—a little wind and noise and some bumps and pockets in the air—a glorious view of the harbour. Then we started to come down. First, I saw the earth directly below through the planes on the left. Then the horizon made a sudden wild lurch and Newport News appeared directly below on my right. This continued for a little while and then we started down at an angle of about 80 degrees to the perpendicular, turning as we went. I later learned that Carlstrom had executed a few steep banks or sharp turns and then spiralled down. It ended with a very pretty landing, following with a series of banks to check speed. Flying from my first impression is a very fascinating game and the one I want to stay with for a while. I have signed up for 100 minutes in the air. While this hundred minutes will not make me a flier by any means I think it is well worth the while in that it gives me a little element of certainty in going abroad. I will know if all goes well that I am not unable to fly.

The next day he wrote:

Two flights this morning, 25 minutes *in toto*. The greatest sport I ever had. Wonderful work. I did most of the work after we got up a safe distance.

Having obtained a certificate of 100 minutes flight and passed the necessary physical examinations, he left for France, arriving at Bordeaux May 31, and soon reported at Avord for training.

Stuart Walcott's Letters

1

Dear H——:

... My work here is going well, although slowly. Those in my class ought to get out by October if nothing goes wrong. There are some 150 Americans learning to fly now in France, besides the ones the Government may have sent over—more than a hundred at this one school, and the oddest combination I've ever been thrown with: chauffeurs, second-storey men, ex-college athletes, racing drivers, salesmen, young bums of leisure, a coloured prize fighter, ex-Foreign Légionnaires, ball players, millionaires and tramps. Not too good a crowd according to most standards, but the worst bums may make the best aviators. There's plenty of need for all of them.

There are lots of Frenchmen here also and a big crowd of Russians, mostly happy youngsters having a very good time. They're always in a hurry to get up in the air and are continually breaking machines and their necks. The Americans have an endless streak of luck in being able to fall out of the air and collect themselves uninjured from amidst a pile of kindling wood which was the machine. As yet I haven't done any piloting in the air, so can't talk very wisely about the glories and thrills of slipping through the ephemeral clouds. All I have learned is that almost any kind of a dub can be a pilot, but that there aren't a lot of very good ones. The idea is to get enough practice to become a good one before arguing with the elusive Boche at a high altitude.

It looks over here as though there would be about two years

more of war, judging from what most people say. It is to be hoped that after twelve to eighteen months we will be able to take France's place at the front, for she deserves to be relieved and will have to be. Even now, France is almost spent; it will be England and the United States who will finish the war. This war is a terrible thing, but for America it is an opportunity as well. I am glad that we have at last come into it and that it will be no halfway fight that we must put up. The Canadians have been about the best regiments in the war. Why shouldn't America be as good? . . .

Stuart.

2

Ecole d'Aviation Militaire
Avord, Cher, France.
Friday, July 13, 1917.

You see it's Friday, the thirteenth, my lucky day, and I'm happy because the work is going well. First, I'll tell you about a smash I had a week or so ago.

The roller or *rouleur* class which I smashed in has the same machine as those that fly with a 45 P motor. Only it is throttled down, and we are supposed to keep it on the ground—just about ready to fly, but not quite getting up—a speed of about 30 m.p.h. When there is the slightest wind we can not roll, because the wind turns the tail around and swings the machine in a circle—a wooden horse—*cheval de bois*. I rode about the end of the list Saturday—and the wind had come up as the day got on. Work stops at 8:30 a. m. always because there's too much wind. My first sortie or trip went O.K. with a considerable breeze on the tail, but on the second there was too much wind and after I got going pretty fast—around she went. The wind caught under the inside wing and up it went. Smash went the outside wheel, and a crackle of busting wood. All the front framework of wood that holds the motor was smashed—a pretty bad break. The monitor was a bit mad and talked to me a bit in French.

The next morning I was called in to see the chief of the Blériot school, Lt. de Chavannes, a very nice officer. He told me that my monitor was not satisfied with me—that he had told me to do something (cut the motor when the machine started to

TWO-SEATER AIRPLANES READY TO ASCEND AT ONE OF THE NEW AMERICAN FLYING SCHOOLS

One method of training the student aviator is by means of the dual control machine. The student takes his place as pilot, while the instructor sits behind him. As long as the student is operating the mechanism correctly he is master of the plane, but the moment he makes a false move the instructor, with duplicate control levers, rights the machine and prevents a spill.

turn) three separate times, and that each time I had intentionally disobeyed, that if anything like that happened again I would be radiated (discharged from the school). That was quite the first I had ever heard of it and I was so mad at the monitor that I could have kicked him in the head. I tried to explain to the lieutenant but he never heard a word, so I just gurgled with wrath and didn't do anything. But yesterday we got another monitor who is a different sort.

The class after *rouleur* is *decollé*—it is the same machine, but one gets off the ground about a metre or two, then slacks up on the motor and settles to the earth. It is strictly forbidden to *decollé* in the *rouleur* class. This morning I had a sortie in the *rouleur* and all of a sudden noticed that I was in the air a bit—managed to keep it straight and get out of the air without smashing. The monitor said nothing so I *decolléed* on all the sorties.

When I got out the monitor explained that it was strictly forbidden to go off the ground in the *rouleur* class, that I shouldn't have done it, and then asked me if I would like to go up to the other class. Whereupon consenting, I am now in the *decollé* class, leaving sixteen rather peeved Americans who arrived in the *rouleur* the same time I did, who can perform in the *rouleur* quite as well as I can and who will remain in the *rouleur* for some time yet. They've no grudge against me, however, as it was only a streak of luck on my part. Later in the morning I had some sorties in the *decolleur* and got up two or three metres. The wind was too strong, so my trips were a bit rough, but nothing was damaged—so hurrah for Friday, the thirteenth.

3

July 17, 1917.
The work has been going very well since last I wrote you, which was only two or three days ago. I told you about at last leaving the blessed roller; I never was so relieved in my life. The &st evening in the *decollé* class, I was requisitioned to turn tails and the morning after there was too much wind to work. The *decollé* is the one where you go up two or three metres and settle down by cutting speed. The first time I had three sorties in the wind, bounced around a lot, but did no damage. The next time was first thing in the morning. Two metres up on the first, four or five on the fifth—strictly against orders. I even had to

piqué—point the machine toward the ground—a little, which is not at all *comme il faut* in the *decollé*. But these Frenchmen are funny chaps—sometimes they will get terribly angry and punish one for disobeying, and again they will be tickled to death with it. If I had smashed while doing more than I was told to, there would have been a lot of trouble; as it was, no objection—and the monitor personally conducted me to the *piqué* class with a very nice recommendation.

Now there are two *piqué* classes: one with a *piste* about a quarter of a mile long, in which one is supposed to do little more than *decollé*, get up about five metres and *piqué un tout petit peu*—hardly at all. After comes the advanced *piqué* with much longer *piste* on which one can get up 100 metres (300 feet). On my first sortie in the *piqué*, I was told to roll on the ground all the way, so continuing my policy, did a low *decollé*. Next I was supposed to do a two metre *decollé*, so went up ten and *piquéd*. Had ten sorties in that class one morning, getting as high as I could—about twenty metres—and went to the advanced *piqué* that night—last night. Four sorties there last night with a machine with a poor motor, so didn't get up over a hundred feet. And this morning I did my first real aviating. There was a bit of wind blowing, so the monitor, Mr. Moses, only let a lieutenant and me go up, as we had gone better than the others last night. First it was a bit rainy and always bumpy as the deuce—air puffs and pockets which require the entire corrective force of the wing warp and rudder to overcome. My last sortie was decidedly active. The wind had developed into a bit of a breeze which is to a Blériot like a rough sea to a row boat. Two or three times I got a puff that tipped the machine 'way over—put the controls over as far as I could and waited. It seemed a minute before she straightened.

The trouble was that the machine was climbing and therefore not going very fast. If I had *piquéd*, it would have corrected quicker. I had no trouble at all in making the landing. Hopping out of the machine, I saw the head monitor rushing over to Mr. Moses on the double, shouting volubly in French and berating him severely. I gathered that he had been watching my manoeuvres, expecting something to fall every instant, and that he strenuously objected to Moses letting me go up. Work stopped there for the morning, and it was very fully explained

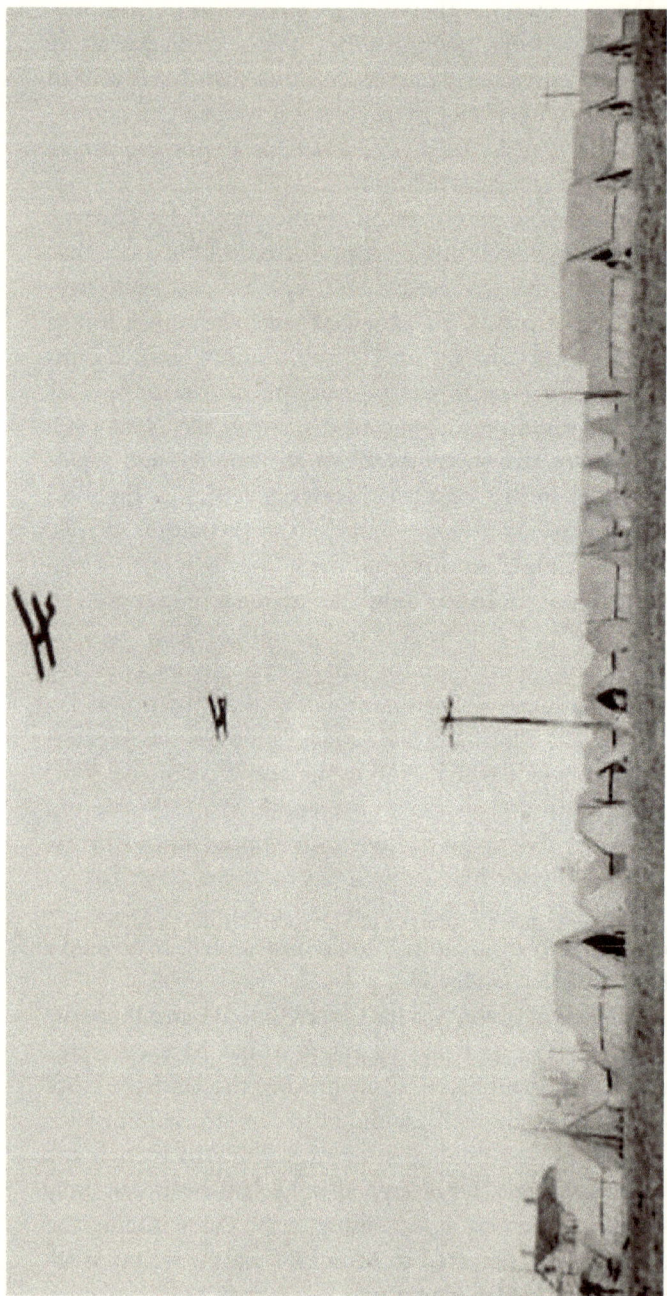

AIRPLANES HOVERING OVER THE TENTS OF TROOPS STATIONED AS A GUARD OF AN AMERICAN AVIATION SCHOOL CAMP

The flying machines and other equipment of our future airmen must be watched day and night to protect them from the tampering of Teuton spies and sympathisers.

to me what the trouble was. If I have some sorties there tonight, I go to *Tour de Piste* (Flying Field) in the morning. I may be on Nieuport in two weeks.

I am now beginning to see the advantages of the Blériot training. There is a great deal of preliminary work on or near the ground. In all other aviation training, such as at Newport News, 90 *per cent* of the work is in making landings—in *piquéing* down, redressing at the proper moment and making gradual connections with the earth. I haven't made a really bad landing yet and the reason is that I have been in a machine so much on and near the ground, that I have sort of developed a sense or feel of it, and almost automatically redress correctly, and settle easily. Also I can tell pretty closely what is flying speed because of the work on the rollers. It's the same way with all the other students only I know it now from my own experience.

And this morning I began to realise that my hundred minutes at Newport News was invaluable. I not only found out some of the tricks of a master hand (Carlstrom) but also developed a bit of confidence in the air, and air sense, without which I could have got into trouble this morning. My bumpy ride this morning is absolutely invaluable. I'll probably never have so much trouble in the air again, because a fast machine or even a Blériot with a good motor, would hardly have noticed these puffs. It was a bit risky, I guess, or the head monitor would not have been worried, but now that it's over, I know a lot more.

4

August 11, 1917.

Dear ———: [1]

You have certainly developed into a wonderful correspondent. Honest-to-goodness, a letter you started my way about a month ago was quite the most satisfactory and amusing thing I've received since I've been over here. Based on practically no material, yet it was alive with interest, every line. There's nothing like a finishing school education. If I thought that you could knit, I would immediately appoint you as my *marraine* (godmother), for it's quite possible for one person to have more than one soldier and I am but a soldier of the second class in the French Army. As I understand it, the chief duty of a *marraine*

1. One of his school friends.

is to write letters—you've started that in good style—and to knit wool scarves, which the devoted soldier hands to a French peasant woman to unravel and make a pair of socks out of. . . . Many Yale boys have wandered in upon us of late, Alan Winslow, Wally Winter, George Mosely, and others. Also Chester Bassett, late of Washington and Harvard University, who I believe has the good fortune to be acquainted with you, a very recommendable young man. They tell me that Cord Meyer is aviating at some camp nearby, but, not having any machines, they have to spend their time touring the country in a high powered motor.

Had a long and gossipy letter from Pat the other day, containing details of many weddings and engagements, even unto young ———— ————.All my classmates are doing the same stunt. How about being original and waiting until the war is over and seeing who of the competitors are left? I quite expect to be, but it's luck I'm trusting to; there's a lot of war left in the nations of Europe. One never can tell; I may come home on permission in a French uniform with a wing on my collar. . . . When the American Air Service is a little further along, it may be that we will be taken over from the French Army.

I finished up in one division of the school the other day and passed to another for brevet, the tests for a military aviator. I sort of have the impression that I wrote you a few weeks ago about it, but not being sure, run the risk of repetition, which, if any, I hope you will excuse. This epistle is being written out at the *piste* (flying field), waiting for the wind to drop enough to fly, and with me seated amidst a bunch of Russians, so if there are any superfluous "*iskis*" or "*ovitches*" in this, you will understand why. The Russians are great fliers; in fact they know so much about it that they never listen to their monitors and as a result break more machines than all the other pupils combined. A month ago five of them went to the next school for acrobacy and in a week every one of them had killed himself. I pulled a bit of the same Russian stuff in the spiral class of the Blériot. All the work is solo—never a flight double command so one has to get instructions on the ground and follow them in the air.

I used my head and senses in performing my first spiral, instead of shutting my eyes, doing what I had been told and trusting to God. The result was that I made one more turn than I expected

24

to and that quite perpendicular, not at all *comme il faut* in a Blériot. Why something did not break has been the wonder of the Blériot school. But nothing did and we got down all right. Another time I planted a cuckoo on her nose, which is not at all encouraged by the monitors. 'Tis quite a trick to balance a monoplane on its nose on the ground, but I did it—quite vertical she lay, with me in the middle struggling with the safety belt and wondering which way it was going to fall. My final appearance in the Blériot school was likewise spectacular. The left wing hit a hole in the air which the right one didn't.

Naturally things tipped; then they wouldn't straighten and the only thing to do was to dive to the low side. I did, but forgot to shut off the motor. A very steep and fast spiral resulted in which I lost 500 feet in a half-turn in about two seconds, I think, all with the motor going to beat the cars. I must have been travelling at many hundreds of miles an hour. Once again nothing broke, but it was no fault of mine that it didn't. . . .

Sincerely,

Stuart.

5

August 25, 1917.

I started for my altitude test three days ago. The requirement is one hour above 2,000 metres. I got to 1,950 metres and one cylinder refused to fire, so I was forced to come down. The next morning I tried again, got to 900 metres and the magneto ceased to function, thereby stopping all progress. I glided toward home, but didn't have quite the height to make the *piste*, so had to land in a nearby field, just dodging a potato patch. A flock of curious sheep came around and carefully examined the machine, getting considerably mixed up in the wires of the open tail construction and leaving considerable wool thereon. When the mechanics eventually got the motor going, I started off, didn't get quite in the air before the motor went bad and then I ran into a bean patch, gathering about a bushel of beans with the same tail wires.

Yesterday morning I tried again, climbed to 2,000 in fourteen minutes and to 3,500 metres (11,500 feet) in forty minutes. I went up through some light clouds and when I got to 8,500, the top of my recording barograph, more clouds had formed and I was practically shut off from the earth, nothing but a beautiful sea of clouds below me, a very beautiful sight. One other machine was in sight, far below me, but on top of the clouds. Not wanting to get lost I came down through the clouds and stayed out my hour just above 2,000 and below the clouds, where the air was very much churned up, keeping me very busy. Just as soon as the time was up I came down with a pair of very chilled feet, making the 2,000 metres in five minutes to the ground. No work since then on account of bad weather.

This morning I attended my first Catholic funeral, that of the commandant of the school who was the victim of a midair collision, a very unusual accident. The other machine got down safely though badly smashed. Everybody in camp attended the funeral in the chapel of the Artillery Camp next door. I understood none of the service, but the music by a tenor and a 'cello was excellent. While the *cortège* was going down the hill to the cemetery, a Nieuport circled overhead very low for half an hour or more and dropped a wreath. It was a very impressive ceremony.

I expect to start on triangle and *petit voyage* in a few days. When they are done, I will be a breveted flier in the French Army. Then comes *perfectionné* work and acrobacy, so it will be quite a while yet for me.

6

August 31, 1917.

Dear ———:[2]

Here it is almost September and I am still a dog-goned *élève pilote*. Verily, every time I think of how the time passes along without results, I go wild. My complaint is caused by the west wind, which has blown about twenty-five days during the month of August and seems likely to continue well on into September. The only variety is an occasional storm. For the past two weeks I've been waiting to start my voyages, two trips to a town forty miles away and back and two other triangular trips about 180 miles long each. When they are done, one becomes a *pilote élève;* and there's a great if subtle difference when the words are reversed.

An *élève pilote* is the scum of the earth, looked down on by

2. One of his school friends.

26

mechanics, pilots, monitors, and everyone else; *a pilote élève* can wear wings on his collar and is as good as anyone else. He is permitted to fly in rough weather, to take chances and is not in so much danger of getting radiated if he gets in trouble. The proper thing to do on a triangle or *petit voyage* is to have something bust directly over a nice *château*; make a skilful landing on the front lawn under the eyes of the admiring household and then be an enforced guest for a few days until one is rescued by a truck and mechanics. One has to be very careful where the *panne de moteur* catches him lest he have to make his landing in a lake or on a forest, which is apt to be a bit awkward. One chap, an American, has been out on a triangle for two weeks, staying at some country place, and there are four others at another school near a big town waiting for weather to return. Reports give us to believe they are having a much better time there than we are here.

Between here and the point for the *petit voyage*—a little bit off the route, is the big future American aviation camp and also an Artillery camp. There are quite a bunch of fellows there, Quentin Roosevelt, Cord Meyer, etc., I think. Every American that has left on his voyages in the last month has stopped there against all orders and been bawled out by the monitor. One has to keep a recording barometer or altimeter machine, a barograph, during the voyages, which indicates all stops. One chap came back home the other day with a barometer record showing beyond the shadow of a doubt that he had made a stop of about fifteen minutes *en route*. The monitor saw it, said, "*Alors*, all you Americans stop off there, I don't like it." Then the chap tried to explain how he had had a *panne* and come down in a field out in the country somewhere, fixed the motor and come on home. He almost got away with it, but the monitor happened to snook around a bit and noticed on the tail very clearly written a good Anglo-Saxon name, the name of the town, and the date—quite indisputable evidence. I fully expect to have a *panne* there myself before long.

By the way, to declare a short pause in my chronicle of aviation, how about all those "letters that are to follow"? If you try to tell me how good you are to your Belgian soldier, I refuse to believe a word until you treat me in the same way. And I also refuse to accept anyone as a *marraine* (isn't that what you call

27

these fairy godmother persons one is supposed to correspond with during the war and marry afterward? How inconsiderate some of them are, to take three or four soldiers, just assuming that not more than one will survive; however, they may be wise to have more than one iron in the fire. But my parenthesis grows apace.)—I say I refuse a *marraine* until she approves her ability. But let me see again. Does said *marraine* have to be a complete stranger? It seems to me that is customary, and also usually they are of different nationalities. All of the foregoing weak line will be interpreted as a mere plea for that other letter. I've never made this *"absence makes the heart grow fonder"* stuff at all. Even ———— has given me up; I remain to her only another of the forgotten conquests (?) of the dead past. . . . .

This odd person, Bassett, wandered in all dressed up like a patch of blue sky and I just had to let you know he was here. With absolute confidence in each other's integrity, we put our loving messages side by each. By the way, he is a good scout, don't you think? I have gotten to like him immensely since he has been here. I never had a better time in my life than one evening in Paris with Chet. However quiet the party, he is the life of it.

It must be that I take my weekly shave—in cold, cold water, with a dull, dull razor. Oh, happy thought! Tell the father and brothers hello from me. Also tell ———— to drop me a line of what he's doing and when he's coming over.

Stuart.

7

September 1, 1917.

The wild man in the Nieuport was out again this morning giving some one a joy ride. There is a long straight stretch of road in front of our *piste* and he came down that several times, a nasty puffy wind blowing which bothered him not at all, flying only two or three feet off the ground. In front of the *piste* is a telephone wire crossing the road. He came along the road 100 miles an hour until almost on top of the wire and jumped up just in time to clear it by a few feet—really beautiful work. He goes all over the surrounding country flying low, hopping over trees and houses, sometimes turning up sideways to slip between two trees a bit too close together to fly through; sometimes dragging a wing through the space between a couple of

SUIT IN USE BY THE UNITED STATES ARMY AVIATORS
The airman cannot be clad too warmly. Recently in an altitude flight an Italian aviator, Lieutenant Guido Guidi, encountered a temperature of 89 degrees below zero at a height of 19,750 feet, but he continued to mount another mile

STUDENT AND INSTRUCTING AVIATORS MAKING NOTES OF FEATS OF
MEN IN THE AIR.

The amounts of actual flying time allotted to a student aviator at a
training school is comparatively brief. A major portion of his instruction
is derived from watching the mistakes of others and in being told how
to remedy his own defects, carefully noted by experts while he is "up."

hangars or doing vertical wages just in front of them. It doesn't seem possible that any man can be so much a part of his machine, can be so consistently accurate that he never misses. For this chap, Lumière, has never had a smash. . . .

A chap named Loughran started off on one of his brevet voyages a few days before I got ready for brevet. He got quite a ways along, ran into a storm, went above it, got caught in a cloud, kept on for quite a long way being drifted by a strong wind, then came down through the clouds and found that they were only 400 feet above the ground. After a while he found a place to land and came down safely. He went to a farmhouse, got his machine guarded and tied down. In the meantime word had spread over the countryside that an aviator had come down there and the entire population came out to look him over. A grand equipage drove up with a count who lived in a nearby *château*. He insisted that Eddie come to the *château* and accept their hospitality.

There the fortunate Ed stayed five days; the countess talked English, and also some house guests. He hadn't brought a trunk so borrowed razor, etc., from the count; went down to see the machine every day in the baronial barouche. Whenever he went to the little town in the vicinity all the kids followed him around the streets and when at last he left, he was presented with a multitude of bouquets and had to kiss each and every donor. He brought back pictures of the *château*—a delightful looking old place—and numerous addresses.

8

September 4, 1917.

At last the two weeks of wind and rain has ceased and now it is perfect weather—a bit of a breeze and lots of sun for the last two days. Yesterday morning there weren't enough machines to go around so I did not work, making the eighth consecutive day I hadn't stepped in a machine. Last evening I at last and with much rejoicing started out on my "maiden voyage" to another school about 60 kilometres away (37.5 miles). It was delightfully easy—nothing to do but climb two or three thousand feet and just sit there and watch the country unfold, comparing the maplike surface of the earth spread out below with the map in the machine. In good weather it is very easy to follow, spot roads, towns, woods, rivers and bridges. Railroad tracks get lost at high altitudes and are harder to find anyway. One has to keep an eye open for a place to land within gliding distance in case of a *panne* always, but the country is so flat and so much cultivated around here that it is absurdly simple. I endeavoured always to keep some pleasant looking house or *château* in range in case of trouble, for the French are proverbially hospitable to aviators *en panne* (lying to, descending).

Coming back yesterday evening, the sun was pretty low and the air absolutely calm, nothing but the drone of the motor and the wind; the only movements necessary an occasional slight pressure on the joy stick to one side or the other to keep the proper direction. I came very nearly going to sleep, it was so peaceful up there; several times closed my eyes and swayed a bit. As a matter of fact one is perfectly safe at that altitude—anything over a thousand feet—because the machine, at least this particular type, won't get into any position from which one cannot get it out within 200 metres at most. But nevertheless I haven't tried any impromptu falls as yet.

This morning I repeated the same identical performance, because for some reason we have to do two *petits voyages*, and had much the same kind of a time as yesterday. On the way home one cylinder quit its job and threw oil instead, covering me from head to foot and clouding up my goggles so I had to wipe them off about every minute. When I got back the mechanics decided that that motor had died of old age and would have to be repaired, so I am again without a machine. Have watched a beautiful afternoon pass by from the barracks when without my luck I'd be working. But with a machine and weather, I can be finished tomorrow; two triangles to do about 200 kilometres (125 miles) each and I can do one in the morning and the other in the evening and then I'm breveted. Perhaps by day after tomorrow I'll start *perfectionné* on Nieuport. I hope so.

9

September 9, 1917.

Since my last to Father, I have had some very interesting times. First, I finished my *brevet* with very little excitement, made all my voyages and only got lost a little bit once. Then I saw two machines on the ground in a field, made a rather dramatic spiral

STUART WALCOTT AT THE FRONT

A TRIO OF PLANES AT A TRAINING CAMP FOR AVIATORS

In the "air colleges," which the government has established recently, the time between matriculation and graduation is measured in months instead of years, but if the period of education is shorter in these schools than in regular colleges the expense is an inverse ratio. A conservative estimate of the cost of training an aviator is from $10,000 to $20.000. Great tracts of land are required for ground schools; many airplanes must be kept on hand, as the breakage is heavy, and repairs are often tedious; motor trucks and motorcycles are necessary subsidiary equipment.

and steeply banked descent amidst a crowd of villagers and got away with it; then found that the machines belonged to two monitors who were bringing them from Paris and had effected a *panne de château*. Being asked what I was doing, I fortunately found a spark plug on the burn and got that repaired. The rest of it was very easy, a bit of flying in the rain which stings the face a bit, but is not bad otherwise.

Since I have been on the Nieuport. There are three sizes of machines on which one is trained, starting with the larger double command and going to the smallest. At Pau, we get another even smaller, about as big as half-a-minute. Four times I went out without a ride—bad weather, crowded class and busted machines, the same old story. Then last night I had my first rides with a monitor who is rather oldish, crabbed and new at his job, a brand new aviator. As you know, when an airplane takes a turn, it does not remain horizontal but banks up: *comme ça* (if you can interpret that illustration—it shows signs of remarkable imaginative power)—*alors*, one banks to take a turn and uses the rudder only a very little because the machine turns along when banked. There is a sort of falling-out feeling the first few times until one becomes a part of the machine.

To get back to the story, this monitor does not like to bank his machine and sort of sidles round the corners, keeping it quite flat and almost slipping out to the outside of the turn. I have done many fool things in a machine and made many mistakes, but never have I been so scared in anything in my life as when riding with this monitor. A monitor is supposed to let the pupil drive as much as he is able, but this bird never let me make a move, and when we got through told me I was too brutal. I was never madder in my life and cursed nice American cuss words all the way home. There's a fifteen kilo ride in a seatless tractor back to camp to improve a bad humour.

Well, this morning I saw some more rides impending and didn't like it, so asked the *chef de piste* to put me with another monitor. He had to know why and I registered my kick, which practically said that the first monitor didn't know his business and couldn't drive, that I was scared to ride with him. The *chef* was a bit sarcastic and told me to take two rides with another monitor to show how I could make a *virage*. I did it the way I've been accustomed to, made a fairly short turn; when we got down, the monitor said "*Epatant*" (Am. "stunning") or something like that to the *chef*. The chef had meanwhile communicated my complaint to the first monitor and he was the maddest man I ever saw. Demanded what "*Ce type là*" (indicating me) wanted, said the *virages* I had just made were dangerously banked (the monitor I was with didn't mind, though) and then all three started arguing at once at me and I spelled all the French I knew. About that time I thought of what you had just told me in a letter about trusting in Latin, which advice and remarks I have come to agree with very much (my admiration for the French has waxed less daily) , and here I realized that I had very successfully made a fool out of a man who was supposed to be my teacher, and he fully resented it.

Then, of all things, the lieutenant, without further remarks, said I was to continue with my first monitor. My heart sank into my feet. I had visions of staying in that class without rides or with only rides and fights for months; I rode no more this morning and what was my delight to find this evening that my bewhiskered pal had left on permission. I got another monitor, a fine one who put his hands on the side of the machine and let me do everything with a bit of assistance on the landing, which is different from what I've been doing on the Caudron. Seven rides and a finish—the twenty-three-metre tomorrow morning. I wasn't very good, but got by.

10

September 14, 1917.
Things for me are going all right. Have made progress on the Nieuport since last I wrote and will fly alone soon. As regards the U. S. Army, things are at a standstill until I get to Paris which will be a week or so. I hope to go to the front in a French *escadrille* and in an American uniform. Some say it can be done; some that it cannot. It sounds so sensible that I am afraid there must be some regulation against it.

11

September 27, 1917.
Since last I wrote a regular letter, considerable has taken place. First, I am now at Pau, having finished up Avord. Have sent postcards to father right along to keep track of movements.

THE TYPE OF TAUBE WHICH MADE THE FIRST AIR RAIDS ON PARIS
This plane, whose outspread tail and rounded wings so closely resemble those of a bird, is too slow to contend with the 1918 type of 125-miles-an-hour machine which is now a common place of the Western Front. It is to the latest speedster warplane what the "one-lunger" automobile of fifteen years ago is to the 12-cylinder racer of today. This style airplane still has its uses in the aviation schools, however.

A SHAM BATTLE IN THE SKY

One of the final tests given a student aviator before he is commissioned as an experienced pilot is a sham battle, in which the newly trained fighting man is given an opportunity to display his ability to outmanoeuvre his opponent and get in position for the "assassination," as the French say.

After *brevet* was over, I did not take the customary permission of forty-eight hours, but went straight to work on Nieuport, D. C. (double command) . One cannot learn a great deal riding with an instructor—only about enough to keep from smashing in landing, because one never knows when the instructor is messing with the controls, when it's one's self. There are five kinds of Nieuports—differing mainly in size, the smaller being faster and more agile in the air, better adapted to eccentric flying. They are 28, 23, 18, 15, 13 (the baby Nieuport). At Avord I had about a week of D. C. on 28 and 23 (the numbers refer to size of wings) with several days of no work. Then some days on 23 alone and finally on 18 alone.

The landings are a bit different from those of the machines I had been flying as they are faster and the machines are quite nose-heavy. In the air the nose-heavy feature makes them "fly themselves"—that is, according to the speed of the motor the machine will rise and climb or *piqué* and descend, with never a touch from the pilot. If the weather is not very bad, the Nieuport will correct itself automatically from all displacements. But in landing the nose-heavy feature causes a great many *capotages*. If the lauding isn't done about right with the tail low—over she goes on her nose or all the way onto her back. It is a very common occurrence and has become almost a joke. When a pupil *capotes*, everybody kids him—no one hurries over to see if he is hurt not at all; he climbs out from under, usually cursing, and in ten minutes the truck is out to salvage the wreck.

It is astounding the way smashes are taken as a matter of course. Yesterday one chap in landing hit another machine, demolishing both but not touching either pilot. Being worth some $15,000 or $25,000, but no one seemed to worry—it's very much a matter of course. The monitor was a little peeved because he will be short of machines for a few days, but that was all. I've seen as many as ten machines flat on their backs or with tails high in the air, on one field at the same time. For myself, I haven't *capoted* or busted any wood since the Blériot days. But I'm knocking on the wooden table now. On several occasions it has been only luck that saved me, as I've made many rotten landings.

Well, to get back to the diary. After finishing at Avord, I waited around for two days to get papers fixed up, requested and obtained permission and then decided not to use it and left straight for Pau after fond farewells to the friends I've been with for three and a half months. Looking back, I didn't have such a bad time at Avord after all, though I did get terribly tired of the living conditions.

My trip to Pau I put down to experience. I discovered one schedule not to travel by in future. Leaving Avord at 2:15 I got to Bourges at 2:45 and found that the train left at 7:29. Fortunately, there was another chap from the school on the train, Arthur Bluthenthal, an old Princeton football star, whom I have gotten to know quite well, so we managed to waste the afternoon together. At 7:29 I started another half hour's journey, at the end of which the timetable said that the train for Bordeaux left at 10:30 (this is all p.m.).

At this town there were some American engineers, so I embraced the fellow countrymen in a strange land. Finished up a not very gay evening by attending the movies, a most odd institution. Clouds of tobacco smoke obscured the screen, and most of the action was around the bar at one side of the hall. Nobody was drunk, but nearly every one was drinking and very gay. This was merely Saturday night in a small town of the Provinces— not in gay Paree. At 10:15 I got in a first class compartment and tried to find a comfortable position in which to sleep. At 2:15 a. m. I had mussed up my clothes considerably, lost my temper and not slept a wink. Then we had to change again. The rest of the morning I sat opposite an American officer, a queer old fogey, and we tried to kid each other into thinking we were sleeping, with no success. Arrived at Bordeaux at 7 a. m., and found that the train for Pau left immediately, so I missed out on breakfast, too—Oh, it was a hectic trip. My idea of a very unpleasant occupation is that of a travelling salesman in France.

12

October 22, 1917.

Ah, ————[3]:

Once more I take my pen in hand to lay at your feet the burdens of an overwrought (how is that word spelled?) mind, said burdens being caused by a most unpleasant captain. Just because I was in Paris for a day and a half without a permission,

3. One of his school friends.

he handed me eight days of jail, and today for nothing at all he hauled me out in front of the entire division and got quite angered when I told him in extremely broken French that I hadn't understood a word. But as the jail doesn't mean anything and doesn't have to be served, I am not worrying very much. The afternoon is misty and there isn't a chance of flying, so he takes particular care that nobody leave the *piste* though there is absolutely nothing to do there, no chance to get warm or comfortable. Which at least gives me a perfect alibi for poor penmanship as I'm sitting in a machine and quite uncomfortable.

Thoughtless creature, so much like the rest of your sex, why did you not tell me where Albert was to be over here, or what he was going to do, or what service he was in, or at least that he was in France? I cleverly deduced the latter from your letter, but did not know where to find him. When I got your letter I was at Pau, not far from Bordeaux (Didn't I write you or postalcard you from there?). Afterward at Paris, I talked to a few very dressed up ensigns with wings on them somewhere (Walker is the only name I remember), and they told me that was near Bordeaux and in the same group with themselves. So if, etc., I might have gone to see the Big Boy.

Yesterday I went to see Billy and another classmate in an artillery camp the other side of Paris. They are officers of the U. S. A. and live as such, which incites in me much envy as I am still a mere corporal of France and treated with no more than my due—not quite as much I sometimes think. That was the expedition that brought the jail. Lots and lots of people are getting over here now. I've seen Heyliger Church and Kelly Craig who are about to become aviators somewhere. Porter Guest just became breveted (that is, a licensed pilot) and was considerably seen in Paris shortly after—no end of college friends are over here and even an occasional American girl is seen in Paris. No friends as yet.

Your letter—I asked at Morgan Harjes about Miss ——— and found that she is at the front in a hospital, so I can't very well find her in Paris. I'm sorry as I would very much have liked to. What one might call permanent people are very nice to know in Paris. I don't know anything

about the front yet, but if I'm near Miss ———'s hospital, will try to get acquainted.

What you said about ——— and his going, I can pretty well

appreciate. There isn't a thing in the world to worry us unmarried and very independent young men over here. If something happens to us, it will bother you all back home a great deal more than us. It's very, very true that women have the heaviest and worst part of war. I had to write a letter the other day to the mother of a pal over here who shot himself when out of his head. A fine pilot and an exceptionally charming fellow, how I pity his poor mother. It's almost unbelievable the number of women one sees in black here in France. Thank God, it can never become that bad at home, for the war will never get so close to us as it has to the French.

I haven't the inspiration to compose an imaginative aeronautic thriller today about the experiences of a boy aviator. Since last writing, have finished Nieuport at Avord, went to Pau and there did acrobacy, came here to Plessis-Belleville and started Spad, now await assignment to an *escadrille* which ought to come within a week. Haven't broken any wood since Blériot days, but have been a bit more rational and done about average good work. The preliminary training is over—combat training doesn't amount to anything till we get to the front. I'll be on a mono-place machine surely. So in my next you can expect to hear mighty tales of combating the Boche at a high altitude. I'm beginning to hear that it's nothing but a lot of routine work, few combats and pretty soon a frightful bore: I refuse to believe it and hang on to romance for all I'm worth.

Give my regards to a whole lot of people and tell them I haven't quite given up all hope of a letter though almost. My friends as a group are not very strong on letter writing. There are only a very few shining exceptions like yourself and verily they do make of me the heart glad.

But enough of this, 'tis bootless, so I sign myself.

Thine as of yore,

Stuart.

13

Escadrille Spa-84,
Secteur Postal 181,
Par A. C. M.—Paris.
November 1, 1917.

Well, I'm here—in sight of the front at last. To date I haven't

LUFBERY AND HIS LIONS WHISKEY AND SODA

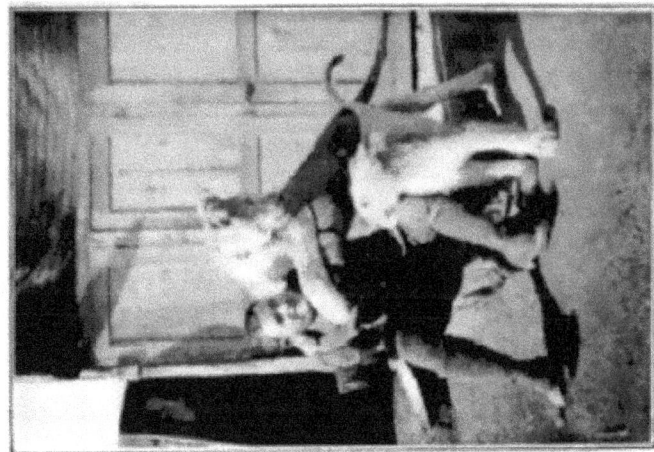

THE LION CUB WHISKEY

LIEUTENANT THAW LEAVES THE GROUND

been out there yet and won't for a few days more as they take lots of care of new pilots and don't feed them to the Boche right away. Probably day after tomorrow the lieutenant in command will take me out to show me around the lines and after that I'll take my place in patrols with the others. The work is exclusively patrolling, establishing as it were a barrage against German machines and preventing as far as possible any incursions of the French lines. As the big attack is over, there is comparatively little activity. Sometimes one goes for a whole patrol without being fired on and without seeing an enemy machine anywhere near the lines. During the three days I've been here, the group has accounted for several Boches without any losses whatever. Young Bridgeman of the Lafayette Escadrille had a bullet through his fuselage just in front of his chest, but suffered no damage except from fright.

There are several *escadrilles* in the group, a *groupe de combat*—it is called—all have Spads which makes it very nice. The Lafayette, 124, is of our group and have adjoining barracks, which makes it very nice (I seem to repeat) for us lone Americans in French *escadrilles*. We drop in there far too often and the first few nights I used the bed of the famous Bill Thaw's roommate, away on permission. Did I write you that one morning he brought in Whiskey to wake me up, and my eye no sooner opened than my head was buried under the covers. Whiskey is a pet—a very large lion cub, which has unfortunately outgrown its utility as a pet and was sent yesterday, with its running mate, Soda, to the Zoo at Paris, to be a regular lion.

They are a very odd crowd—the members of the Lafayette Escadrille, a few nice ones and a bunch of rather roughnecks. Their conversation is an eye opener for a new arrival. Mostly about Paris, permissions, and the rue de Braye, but occasionally about work and that *is* interesting. Nonchalant doesn't express it. When Bridgy got shot up as mentioned above, they all kidded the life out of him and when he got the *Croix de Guerre*, they had him almost in tears—just because he's the kiddable kind.

But in talking about the work—for instance, Jim Hall: "I *piquéd* on him with full motor and got so dam close to him that when I wanted to open fire I was so scared of running into him that I had to yank out of the way and so never fired a single shot."

Or Lufberry just mentions in passing that he got another Boche this morning, but those —— observer people won't give him credit for it. He has fourteen official now and probably twice as many more never allowed him. Some days ago during the attack he had seven fights in one day, brought down six of them and got credit for one. Which must be discouraging.

14

Well ——————[5]

Here I find myself writing to you without waiting for the usual two or three months to elapse. Do you realise that it was over five and a half months ago that I left my native land? It doesn't seem near so long to me. Just at present I have about thirteen hours a day to write, read the *Washington Star* and *New York Times*, eat an occasional meal (we only get two over here, worse luck), build fires in the stove and stroll for exercise. The rest of the time is devoted to sleep. A terribly hard life that of an aviator on the western front! No *appels* (meaning roll calls), discipline or inspections. Only, if there should happen to be a good day, one might be wanted to fly a bit. So far (I have only been out here a week) we have had perfectly ideal aviators' weather—nice low misty clouds about 800 or 400 feet up, which quite prevent aerial activity and yet one is not bothered by mud or depressed by rain. In the morning, one awakes, pokes his head out the window, says "What lo! more luck, a nice light *brouillard*," and closes the window for a few hours more of sleep. Really I have done more resting the past week than most people do in a lifetime!

To get statistical, I finished up at Pau (from where I sent to you a letter, *n'est-ce-pas?*) a month ago, and then spent two very unpleasant weeks at Plessis-Belleville near Paris, at the big *dépot* for the front, waiting to be sent to an *escadrille*, with nothing to do but a little desultory flying, nurse the system, food, weather, lodging, discipline, etc. Eventually my turn came and, with another American, I was dispatched to Esc. SPA 84, where we arrived after the usual delay passing through Paris. That's one nice thing about this country: all roads lead to Paris. Sent from one place to another, it is a safe wager that one goes *via* Paris, and

5. One of his school friends.

46

JAMES NORMAN HALL

always takes forty-eight hours there and gets permission for it if he can. There are a few Frenchmen there still, but on the streets one sees almost entirely American, British or British Colonial officers—occasionally a French aviator and of course clouds of sweet and innocent young things—yes? Nearly all of my class-mates are over here and get to Paris every once in a while, so all I have to do is to sit at the Café de le Paix and if I wait long enough, someone I know will surely come along.

Well, to get back on the track, we eventually found ourselves members of *le-dit* Esc. SPA 84—one *esc.* of a *groupe de chasse*, which means that we will have patrolling work to do mainly and not protection of observation or photo machines—which they tell me, is fortunate. Also we have good machines—the best there are, which might not have happened had we been sent to another type of *escadrille*—purely good fortune. The much advertised Lafayette Esc. No. 124, is a member of the same group, is located near us and does the same work, which makes it much pleasanter for lone Americans. We use their stove and tea of an afternoon quite freely as our quarters are new and not fixed up.

But say, when we do get going, everybody will be in to see us. We'll have a cosy, beautifully wallpapered room clustering around a stove. . . . . The men of 124 are a rather good crowd—not much different from any crowd of Americans, a bit rough but most of it affected because they're away from home, very hospitable, rather daredevil or hardhearted (whichever you wish to call it—the way they talk about each other's narrow escapes, coming falls, the mistakes or misfortunes of departed brothers, and there have been several) and very mixed, centring around Lieutenant Bill Thaw, of the French Army, who impresses me as being very much of a leader and an unusually fine type. There is one tough nut from a Middle Western Siwash-like college, who was probably still ungraduated at 27, and a quiet, innocent looking kid who seems to have just got out of prep school; of course, the tough guy tears the little one.

Then there are a couple of old *Légionnaires*—rather superior and terribly tired of war, quite unenthusiastic, but I dare say congenial when one gets under their hide or fills it full of booze. And Jim Hall, the author chap—quiet, reserved, almost simple in his lack of affectation and boyish in his enthusiasm.

(Gad, how he wants to get his Boche and he almost thinks he did the other day, but it wasn't verified. He followed him down from 1,500 to 200 metres, shooting all the time, and thinks he must have brought him down). . . .

I mention above that I am at present in the status, practically, of a non-flying member? On arriving at the front, one is not rushed straightway to the cannon's mouth, but rather allowed to get acclimated a bit first, to have a few preliminary voyages to look around, etc. During my week here, there has been little flying and I haven't even seen the front, only heard the guns occasionally. Of my three flights, two were just short *tours de champs*. But the other: never in my wildest Blériot days did I do a wilder one. Coming from Pau where I had tried some stunts, I thought I was a bit of an acrobat, second only to Navarre, Guynemer and a few others. So arriving at a safe height, I started to go through the *répertoire*. First came a loop which got around to the vertical point—a quarter turn and then slipped, ending in a vertical corkscrew or climbing barrel turn or whatever you want to call it—then losing momentum and just naturally tumbling. I didn't know what was going on—only that it wasn't right; they told me afterward.

After that came the *renversements* and vertical turns, etc., and not a thing came out. Lost—I got lost thirty times and had to hunt all around to see where I was. Nothing went right and I kept getting madder and madder and poorer and poorer. They were all laughing down below and wondering what was going on up there. Eventually the party ended—one of the old pilots told me that that one flight equalled about thirty hours over the lines and the commander advised against a repetition of the performance, and so I went and lay down. Two hours later I began to feel that perhaps I could stand on my feet again; did you ever have *mal-de-mer*?

So now I really ought to begin to learn something, having acquired that all essential first knowledge of ignorance, which all good students should have. And in the meantime perhaps I shall go and combat the Wily Hun. Said W. Hun need not worry about my bothering him if he doesn't keep fooling around under my nose till I'm ashamed not to go after him. I'm not bloodthirsty a bit, especially till I learn to fly, and the lack of combats isn't going to keep me awake nights for a while yet.

Le Féquant, Thenault, Thaw, Lufbery

RAOUL LUFBERY POSING IN HIS NIEUPORT. TWO FRENCH SERGEANTS ARE ALSO SEEN, ONE HOLDING THE MASCOT WHISKEY.

GUYNEMER

But the bunkmate seems to have gone to bed; it's almost ten—a most unprecedented hour for me to be up, so the end approaches. Kind remembrances as usual—use your discretion and don't forget that long tale of 'Washington Social Tid-Bits' you spoke of—gossip if you prefer. . . .

As ever,

Stuart.

The Next Day.

Addenda:

Your letter on just arriving home has been with me some time and truly brought joy to my heart in this desolate land. (The "desolate" seems to fit in though not applying to the land in question at all.) . . .

Chester Snow is aviating under the auspices of the U. S. Government. I last heard from him in a postal written on the last stop of the last triangle of his brevet, so he should be through training before much longer. The other Chester, Bassett, is still at Avord, so I can not deliver your note to him. . . .

Your other question referred to the army I am in, and is easily answered by saying that the U.S.A. has as yet done nothing but talk about taking us over, "Us" now refers to upward of 200 Americans, I think, either in French *escadrilles* or well advanced in the French schools. Constantly all summer, we have been "going to be transferred in two weeks."

Another quiet, non-flying, slightly rainy day has passed. This isn't perhaps the most ideal spot in the world for a winter resort, from the point of view of comforts, but, considering the ease of conscience because one is not in the position to be called *embusqué*, it is really not half bad. It's starting to rain again rather harder; I wonder if the roof will keep out water?

Yours, etc.,

B. S. W.

15

November 10, 1917.

Evening.

You know November in France. I've been here almost two weeks now and am still *à l'entrainement*, that is, I haven't started in to do any regular work yet. Only five times have I been able to fly in two weeks. But I've got my own machine, and mechanic, everything is in order and I've been assigned to a patrol the last two mornings when it rained. Tomorrow again at 8:50 with four others—patrol for one hour and fifty minutes at about 15,000 feet, back and forth over our sector, sometimes over our own lines, sometimes in Bochie. I'm getting very impatient to get started. In what few flights I've had, I've been working on acrobacy a bit and am gradually learning a few simple things; twice I stayed up a little too long and had to lie down a few hours afterward, almost seasick.

I like Spa 84 very much indeed. The Frenchmen there are much more regular fellahs than most of those I've been with in the schools.

Wertheimer, a sergeant, is a sort of informal and unadmitted chief of the *sous-officiers*. It is he that speaks English and has helped us a lot in getting settled, etc. Very much of a gentleman he is, and understands a bit Anglo-Saxon customs and eccentricities, always gay and an indefatigable worker. We have all been arranging the one big room of our barracks-dining room, reading room, and probably eventually American bar. The walls are covered with green cloth, green paper (of two different shades and neither quite the same as the cloth) , red cloth (on top as a sort of frieze) and red paper. The ceiling is done in white doth to keep in heat and lighten the room. A monumental task it has been, especially as materials are hard to get and expensive. Wertem (as Wertheimer is called) and Deborte have done most of the work. Deborte is also *chef de popote*, which means housekeeper, and a very efficient man.

For four *francs* per day we are fed amazingly well, especially when one realizes that we are near the front in a country which has had three years of war. Deborte hasn't the pleasantest manner in the world at times, but usually is very agreeable, willing to tell me things about flying or the *escadrille*, always ready to work, and a dependable man in the air. And Verber who rooms with Wertem,—he speaks a little English, has a great deal of trouble understanding it, but is picking up. Wears a monocle all the time because he's got a bum eye, carries a stick and has an extremely eccentric appearance, but withal is very agreeable and a very valuable man. He has the habit of taking long trips all alone far into Germany just to see what is going on. Pinot is the name of the little roly-poly chap everybody calls

WAR CROSS WITH PALM,
AWARDED IN RECOGNITION OF
WALCOTT'S SERVICES

Bul–Bul, who used to be a mechanic and now is a very good, merry pilot.

He has a great *pension* toward Pinard, is violently but not at all objectionably non-aristocratic, is forever laughing or kidding someone, walks on his hands to amuse people, and is the delight of all the *mécanos*. Demeuldre is a very quiet sort of schoolboy type who has been a pilot of biplanes and reconnaissance machines for a long time. He came to the *escadrille* recently with a record of two Boches as pilot of a biplane (that is, his machine gun man did the shooting and they both get credit), and a few days ago brought down a German in flames, his first as *pilote de chasse*. There are two others away on permission, whom I don't know yet.

16

Somewhere in France,
November 13, 1917.

Dear Father:

Campbell was in the Lafayette Escadrille and they are a member of the same group as Spa 84, so I have asked them about him. He was on a patrol with another chap, They attacked some Boches and when it was over the other chap was alone. Campbell was brought down in German territory and so reported missing. I believe that the chap he was with has seen and talked to Campbell's father or some close relative since. Another chap named Bulkley was brought down in similar circumstances about the first of September. Ten days ago, word was received from the American Embassy that he had communicated with them, a prisoner in Germany. There are many similar cases, where men brought down with crippled machines or wounded escape destruction by a miracle. The only sure thing is when a machine goes down in flames or is seen to lose a wing or two.

For instance, there are two officers in the group who are in the best of health and daily working. Several months ago, they were on patrol together, collided in the air. One cut the tail rigging completely off the other and they separated, one without a tail and the other with various parts of a tail mixed among the cables and struts of one side of his machine. They both landed in France, one on his wheels followed by a *capotage* or somersault turnover, the other quite completely upside down. Then a term in the hospital and back they are again. Kenneth Marr, an American, had the commands of both his tail controls cut in a combat, the rudder and elevator, leaving him nothing but the *aileron*—the lateral balance control and the motor. He landed with only a skinned nose for casualties and got a decoration for it.

Another chap in an attack on captive balloons, *drachens*, dove for something like 10,000 feet *vertically* and with *full motor* on, thereby gaining considerable speed as you can imagine. He came right on top of the balloon, shot and to keep from hitting it, yanked as roughly as he could, flattening out his dive in the merest fraction of a second. Imagine the strain on the machine! When he got home, all the wires had several inches sag in them; the metal connections of the cables in the struts and wood of the wings had bit into the wood enough to give the sag.

Machines are built to stand immense pressure on the under side of the wings. In some acrobatic manoeuvres I was trying the other day, I made mistakes and caused the machine to stall and then fall in such a way that the full weight was supported by the *upper surface*—by the wires which in most machines are supposed merely to support the weight of the wings when the machine is on the ground. Yes, the Spad is a well built machine, the nearest thing to perfection in point of strength, speed and climbing power I've seen yet. Of course it's heavy and that's why they put 150-280 HP in them. The other school, that of a light machine with a light motor—depending for its success on lack of weight rather than excess of power, may supplant the heavier machine in time—I can't tell. So, as anyone who knows has said right along, there is a long way to go in the development of the J N or even the little tri-plane, before American built planes get to the front. Of the bombing game, I don't know anything at all.

Yesterday there was a revue here in honour of Guynemer, and decorations for the pilots of the group who had won them. Three Americans received the *Croix de Guerre*—members of the Lafayette Escadrille. Lufberry, the American ace, carried the American flag presented to the *escadrille* by Mrs. McAdoo and the employees of the Treasury Department—besides the two aviation emblems of France. He was called to receive his decoration "for having in the course of one day held seven combats,

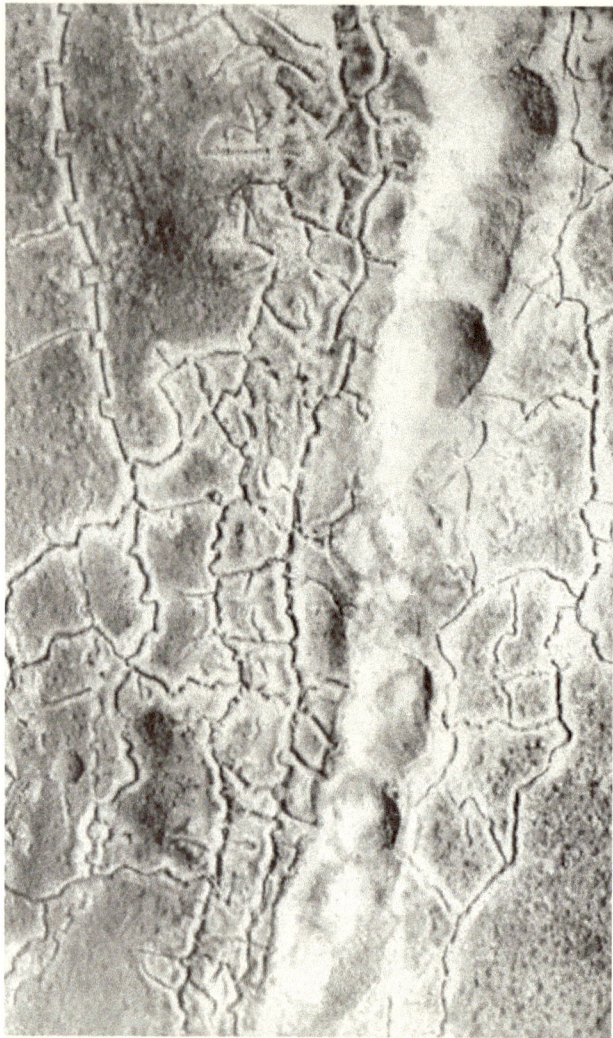

A VIEW OF THE GERMAN FIRST AND SECOND LINE TRENCHES ON THE WESTERN FRONT: FROM A PHOTOGRAPH TAKEN AT AN ELEVATION OF 3,300 FEET.

The most conspicuous features of this warscape—the five deep depressions in the lower half of the photograph are not shell craters; they are the scars left by the explosion of mines under enemy listening posts which had been dug out into No Man's Land. In studying aerial photographs it is usually easy to distinguish between the Germans and French lines from the fact that the German system almost invariably consists of two well-defined lines of trenches, while the French have one, a first line with numerous irregular ramifications.

descended one German plane in flames, and forced five others to land behind their lines" (which means that he is officially credited with one, his thirteenth, and that the other five though probably brought down, do not count for him because there were not the necessary witnesses required by the French regulation). Being the bearer of the flag, he was a very worried man to know what to do with the flag when he should go up to get his medal, till one of the fellows in 124 (the Lafayette) came to his rescue.

For a military *revue* it was decidedly amusing. Aviators are not very military. The chief of one of the *escadrilles* was commissioned to command the mechanics who are plain soldiers with rifles and steel helmets for the occasion. He is a bit of a down and amused the entire gathering, kidding with the officers. The pilots of each of the five *escadrilles* were in more or less formation, most of them with hands in their pockets for it was chilly, and presenting a mixture of uniforms unparalleled in its heterogeneity. Every branch of the service represented and endless personal ideas in dress. Because of the occasion, *repos* has been granted to the entire group for the afternoon, another group taking over our patrols. So that after the *revue*, everyone had the afternoon to waste—a sunny day which is quite unusual this month. Within a half hour, every machine that was in working order was in the air—forming into groups and then off for the lines, just looking for trouble—a voluntary patrol they call it. Which opened my eyes a bit to the spirit in the French service after three years of war.

Word from Paris that those Americans in the French service who have demanded their release to join the U. S. A. have obtained that release—which probably means that all we wait for now . . . is the commissions.

This afternoon I took another trip with one of the old pilots to look over the sector. We stayed over France and didn't get into trouble although there were lots of Bodies around. Hope to get really started soon An amusing one this morning: two pilots from the group were on patrol and attacked a single German about two kilometres behind the German lines. They completely outmanoeuvred him, he got cold feet and started for the French lines, giving himself up. The funniest part about it is that the machine gun of one of the attackers was jammed and he couldn't possibly have hurt the Boche—just had the nerve to stay and throw a bluff. They dome back to camp just before dark this evening, one of them flying the German machine and the other guarding him in a Spad. The machine is an Albatross monoplane (biplane)—finished in silver with big black crosses on the wings and tail—a really beautiful thing. It flew around camp for several minutes before landing. It is the second machine that has been scared down since I've been out here.

17

At the Front,
Somewhere in France,
November 17, 1917.

At present things are hopelessly slow on account of bad weather, so I have a good deal of time to write and naught to write of. I still am waiting for my baptism of active service which is assigned for each day and held up on account of fog, low clouds or rain. In the afternoon it usually lifts a little, not enough to fly over the lines, but sufficient to permit a little *vol d'entrainement*, a practice flight around the field. I've been taking every chance to learn to fly, practicing *reversements*, vertically banked turns, 90° nose dives, etc.

Two day ago, we had a very interesting mimic combat in the air. The Boche machine, which has been captured, and a Spad, both driven by very clever pilots, manoeuvred for position during fifteen or twenty minutes at 1,000 feet or less, back and forth over the field, doing ahnost every possible thing in the air—changing direction with incredible rapidity, diving, climbing, wing slipping, upside down dives—everything under the sun.

Two of them were at it again today in two Spads, just manoeuvring. What a lot there is to learnt When I got through acrobacy at Pau, I had the impression that that kind of stuff was relatively easy—now I know different. For the present I'm working on the system of try one thing at a time—get that fairly well and then commence another. And small doses—ten or fifteen minutes for an acrobatic flight, not more, because one can easily get dangerously sick in a very short time. Not that there is any particular peril in getting ill in the air, only it's beastly uncomfortable!

LIEUTENANT DOUGLAS CAMPBELL

PRESENTATION OF THE FLAG TO LAFAYETTE ESCADRILLE

PRESENTATION OF THE FLAG TO LAFAYETTE ESCADRILLE

18

At the Front—Somewhere in France.
November 30, 1917.

The rumour at the Lafayette Escadrille this evening is that they have been at last transferred. Of course they had similar rumours many times before. For myself I am becoming rather indifferent, very well satisfied here except for weather, and getting what I came over here for.

Father mentioned something about a monitor's job (after I had had experience at the front). My present inclination is decidedly against the idea. There is no job in the world I like less to think of and there are plenty of people who want to get comfortably settled in the rear, so let them, say I, and may they enjoy it. It is not a very pleasant job. As a retirement after a period of service at the front it is another matter. Of all people I can think of I have the smallest right to an *embusqué* job at present—so here I hope to stay. Whether I fly with an American or French uniform I don't care very much at the present moment. I had rather get a Boche than any commission in the army, but one cannot always tell about the future; perhaps after a few good scares I'll be ready to jump at a monitor's job.

19

At the Front,
December 1, 1917.

I tried to give you all some idea of the strength of a Spad in a letter a while ago. At home people speak of a factor of safety, meaning the number of times stronger the machine is than is necessary for plain flying. The Spad is made so that a man can't bust it no matter what he does in the air—dive as far and as fast as he can and stop as brutally as he can—it stands the racket. Of course, motors do stop and if it happens over a mountain range—well, that's just hard luck.

Have had a few patrols since last I wrote. One at a high height, 4,000-4,500 metres, considerably above the clouds which almost shut out the ground below, wonderfully beautiful sight but beastly cold, and a couple when the clouds were low and solid. The patrol stays at just the height of the clouds, hiding in them and slipping out again to look around. If it gets below, the enemy anti-aircraft guns pepper it whenever near the lines and at a low altitude that is rather awkward—so the patrol shows itself as little as possible.

It's lots of sport to try to keep with the patrol: be behind the chief of patrol, see him disappear and then bump into a fog bank, a low-hanging cloud and not see a dam thing. Then dive down out of the cloud wondering whether the other guy is right underneath or not; shoot out of the cloud and see him maybe 500 yards away going at right angles. Then bank up and turn around fast and give her the gear—full speed to catch up and so on. See a Boche regulating artillery fire, start to manoeuvre into range and zip I he's out of sight in the clouds and the next you see he is beating it far back of his lines. Not very dangerous this weather, but lots of fun.

20

December 3rd, 1917.

Dear ——————[6]:

Thanks for the merry, merry wishes for the gay Xmas season and I'll try to remember them when the day comes along. Sundays and holidays are not very much noticed here at the front, except that on Sunday the mechanics all get full of *pinard* and song and devilment—the *pinard* (meaning cheap red ink used by the French in place of drinking water) is of course responsible for the two latter. In the villages, the entire male population likewise drinks much wine and everyone—man, woman, child, dog, and domestic animal, parades the streets—dressed up all like a picture book (applying mostly to women and children). Occasionally they cross the sidewalk, but the middle of the street is *the* place to walk.

One Sunday, I went to church, the first time since last Easter, I think, to attend the mass given for the departed brethren of the *escadrille*. The chapel is in a little town a few miles from our camp. Along in the Middle Ages or anyway a long time ago, there was a beautiful cathedral there—now the town is insignificantly small. The front of the cathedral is standing almost in its entirety and the walls for a little way back, dwindling down into glorious ruins and finally tumbled masses of rock and stray pillars. Where the back wall once stood, there now runs a little brook (I almost called it bubbling, but it happens to be an

---

6. One of his school friends.

unusually dead and not over-clean little stream). The chapel is a place about as big as a minute, snuggling in beside the big front wall of the ancient cathedral. The service was meaningless to me—what wasn't Latin was French. I followed the fellow in front of me and didn't miss it once on the getting up and down (fortunately, *militaires* don't have to kneel, I suppose because they appreciate the fact that most of them wear breeches made by French tailors).

But they fooled me once. What must have been the village *belle* (what a village!) passed a little button bag affair in baby blue ribbon, and gathered up the *shekels*. I dropped mine in and horror—here comes the young sister with an identical bag and asks for more and I was unprepared and had to turn her down amidst my blushes. I thought she was working on the other side of the house as we used to do at evening service and to this day I don't know why they took up two collections though it has been explained to me three times in French.

Have had some very pleasant trips over the German border (present, not 1914), have watched a few Archies bursting at a safe distance away and seen some specks which were Boche planes, but am not ready to write a book yet. Yesterday morning we had the first sortie at 6:45 daylight. A solid bank of clouds over the camp here at 2,000 metres. The lines are parallel to a river and a few kilometres north. The edge of the cloud bank was over the river, sharp as if cut by a knife and all Germany cloudless. We slipped out from under it and back on top just in time to see the sun get over the horizon—almost as far away as Rheims, which we just cannot see. The river and canal were just silver ribbons on a black cloth stretching for miles due east. Under us we could make out the ground on one side and the clouds on the other, and to the west the cloud bank continued to follow the lines, a gloriously beautiful panorama. The cloud bank stayed nearly the same the two hours we were up. From a distance above or below, a cloud is just a big, soft, quiet cushion of cotton fluff, but near to it is a seething, irregular, tossing, furious jumble of mist.

We saw a few Boches, far behind their lines. An hour after we were back, they said that Lufbery had just brought down another machine, his 15th, in flames. He was using a new machine and the gun was not properly regulated—seven balls were in each blade of the propeller, yet it held together and brought him home. I was down at the Lafayette hangars talking to Bill Thaw, and here comes the mighty man in a hurry from reporting his flight. With fire in his eye he got in his old machine and off again for the lines. At noon he had brought down another, which hasn't yet been officially *homologué*, but is none the less sure for that. Thaw brought down one this morning. They are doing well, these men of the American Escadrille—still French, however, though shortly to be transferred, we hear.

May your Xmas be a happy one, and the new year and those to follow bring you ever better fortune than the last one.

Stuart.

21

Châlons-sur-Marne.
December 8, 1917.

Dear ———[7]:

I got the Sunday *Star* a few days ago and there was that same old picture and ——— staring me in the face! A very nice write-up, I thought it. What a bunch of big-wigs they did gather together! We packed up bag and baggage yesterday and flew off to a new place, and here we are waiting for the baggage to catch up. I have grave fears that there may be some fighting one of these days, and if so, I think it will be about time for me to get out of this war. Cheery oh!

Stuart.

22

Châlons sur Marne.
December 8, 1917

Yesterday we were awakened at 6 and told that we were going to move out, bag and baggage at 2. So now as new barracks were not ready we came down here last night and have been seeing the sights of the town since. It is full of Americans, ambulances, doctors, Y. M. C. A. workers, everything but fighting men which I trust we'll see before long.

Stuart.

---

7. One of his school friends.

The Final Combat

On December 12, while on patrol, Stuart Walcott met a German biplane carrying two men. Three cable reports agree that he shot down and destroyed this machine about two and a half miles within the German lines. He then started back for the French lines and was overtaken by four Albatross German planes. He was overcome and his machine went down in a nose dive within the German lines, it being assumed that either he was shot or his machine disabled.

There was still a hope that he might have escaped death. Inquiries were at once instituted through the American Red Cross and the International Red Cross, with the result that on January 7 a cable came from the International Red Cross stating that it was reported in Germany that S. Walcott was brought down during the afternoon of December 12 near Saint Souplet, and that he was killed by the fall.

On January 11 the French Government awarded the *Croix de Guerre* to the fallen flyer, with the accompanying citation:

Corporal Walcott, an American, who volunteered for the duration of the war, and a young pilot of admirable spirit and courage, on December 12, 1917, attacked an enemy airplane. He pursued it four kilometres behind the German lines, where he brought it down. He was in turn attacked by three other monoplanes and was driven down.

The medal was received on his behalf by members of his squadron and has been forwarded to his father, Dr. Charles D. Walcott. Secretary of the Smithsonian Institution, Washington.

Stuart Walcott

(A biographical note written by his father.)

Benjamin Stuart Walcott was sturdy and self-reliant as a boy and very early developed strong personal initiative, good sense and courage. I find in my notebook under an entry of July 6, 1905, a few days before Stuart's ninth birthday, that with him and his brother Sidney I had measured a section of over 10,000 feet in thickness of rock with dip compass and rod in northern Montana, and that that night we slept out on the Continental Divide after a sandwich apiece for supper. On July 16, "Went up the Gordon Creek with Stuart and cut a few trees out of the trail." And on the next day, "Stuart assisted me in collecting fossils from the Middle Cambrian Rocks."

In 1906 Stuart helped in gathering Cambrian fossils in central Montana, and in recognition of his effective work one of the new species of shells was named after him, *Micromitra (Paterina) stuarti.*

He also assisted in British Columbia in geological work during the summer of 1907, and in 1908, when twelve years old, he was placed with one packer in charge of a pack train operating in what is now the Glacier Park, Montana, and in southern British Columbia. On this trip one morning I heard faint rifle shots, and upon overtaking the pack train found Stuart shooting away with a 22 gauge rifle at a grizzly bear, which was some distance down the slope below the trail. On reminding him of the danger, he said he wanted to drive the bear away to prevent a stampede of the animals.

Both at home and in school his actions were largely influenced by a determination first to know what was the right thing to do, and guided by this habit, when it looked as though the United States would enter the European War, he decided that it was his duty to take part in it. When the *Lusitania* was sunk he felt strongly that the United States should take a positive stand in favour of the freedom of the seas, that the rights of Americans should be protected even if it meant war, and he was ready to fight for it.

In common with the majority of the youth of America, he had the feeling that it was a patriotic duty and privilege to offer personal service to the Nation when its ideals and motives were assailed by a foreign foe. He first offered his services to the Signal Corps and received a temporary appointment. Realising that training as an expert aviator could be more quickly obtained in France than in this country, he went to France and enlisted in the French Army with the expectation of being transferred later to the American forces. This would have been done prior to his being shot down within the German lines on December 12, had he not been awaiting action by the United States Aviation Service in France in examining and arranging for the transfer of the American aviators in the French Army to the service of the United States.

Throughout his life the dominating thought was to be of positive service wherever he might be placed. At the same time he was thoroughly a boy and enjoyed a frolic and fun as much as any one of his companions.

He prepared for college at the Taft School, expecting to enter Yale, and passed the examinations for that university before he was sixteen. Upon further consideration he selected Princeton, largely because of the preceptorial method of training, and was a senior when he decided to enter the service of his country.

Stuart was an unusually well balanced boy and youth; his moral convictions were sound, definite, and expressed by action rather than words.

Charles D. Walcott.

The American Spirit

LIEUT. BRIGGS KILBURN ADAMS R.F.C.

Contents

Preface

In the autumn of 1916 among the seventy or eighty students enrolled in a course in English Composition that I was giving at Harvard University was Briggs Kilburn Adams. For some time he remained only a name to me; yet in the themes that bore his name I soon found myself taking a special interest. For they revealed two facts about him: he had spent the previous summer driving an ambulance in France, and he had unusual ability to describe what he had seen and felt.

When he came to me for a conference, I recognised in him the boy who had been sitting in the front row and looking up at me during my occasional talks to the class, with an expression embarrassingly intent—relieved now and then from any suggestion of over-appreciation by a flicker, equally embarrassing, of quizzical humour. He was tall and well built and handsome; his bluish-gray eyes were shaded by long, curling eyelashes, his mouth had a gentle, sensitive curve, his fingers were long and slender, indicating the excellent musician that he was; he spoke in a low, rather slow voice, and seemed an attractive combination of shy reticence and willingness to be drawn out. He told me a little about his work in France—how he had driven wounded at four miles an hour and suffered because he knew that even then the slight bumping over rough places was agonising to them. The fine sensitiveness of a gentle and sympathetic nature showed in his talk, as always in his writing.

But none of his work at this time had the quality of thought and style to be found in the letters to the dearly-loved members of his family after he had begun to fly. As I wrote to his father when a few of these letters first appeared in the *Harvard Alumni Bulletin*:

> He never wrote anything for me which could compare with these letters, and nothing else that has been written about the war, that I have read, can compare with them. They are the

most beautiful bits of writing that have come out of the war—beautiful in style and colour and motion. No one else has taken me up in the air and shown me what it must be to fly; no one else has presented so vivid a figure of war as it should be portrayed. And the little touch about perhaps finding his lost sister Carol 'on the other side of the next cloud,' is one of those wonderful bits of simplicity and imagination that come only to the gifted and are to be found only in great literature.

What could be finer than the passage in that notable letter to his mother in which he writes:

I go about, as it were, hands with palms out, all about my heart, holding things outside of it. I am conscious of things I don't like, or discomforts sometimes . . . but I won't let them get into the inside where they hurt. If I can change them, I can do it just as well keeping them outside, and if I can't change them,—well, what does it matter?—they're outside.

As a Harvard professor said of this passage, it is the historic "*They shall not pass*," as applied to personal life.

Professor Francis G. Peabody, of Harvard, writing to Major Adams, said of the letters printed in the *Harvard Alumni Bulletin* shortly after Lieutenant Adams's death, that:

They are not only gallant and beautiful in their feeling, but singularly elevated in their style, as though his new experience had lifted him into new levels of expression and given to his language something of the clearness and freshness of the upper air. All who love or serve Harvard University—and indeed all lovers of noble young men—must read these letters with a renewed sense of spiritual education, which the tragedies of the time are providing, and will share the happy pride with which you must think of his short but complete career.

At the time when my acquaintance with Briggs Adams began, his interests had awakened and were reaching out in many directions. His love of nature, of literature, and of music—he was a leader of the 'Varsity musical clubs in many of their concerts—was alive and growing. He liked to experiment with verse-forms, to analyse the mood inspired by a symphony, to record the impressions received in a walk through the woods. But in his themes and in his talk he kept reverting, of course, to the one great theme—the war. He had come back from France, passionately longing to see his country in the war, passionately longing to take an active part in the war himself. Indeed, before leaving France to return to complete his college education, he had enrolled for service the following year in the Lafayette Escadrille.

In April, 1917, he finished with college—as did so many other ardent youths. His first efforts to enter the aviation service met with failure. How well he finally succeeded is revealed in his letters and testified by his comrades. He graduated first in a class of twenty with an average of 94, the highest mark that had been achieved up to that time. A fellow cadet wrote of his flying in England before he had won his lieutenant's commission as follows:—

> Our boys here—the seven who came with me—are ready for instruction on the 'real' machines —— fighting buses. B. K. Adams, who is a splendid flyer, has already graduated, and will go to —— soon. He gave one of the finest exhibitions I have seen and boosted our stock 100 *per cent*. He was taken 'dual' on this 'real' machine, and after only ten minutes' instruction, and one landing, he said he could 'fly it alone.' Permission was granted, and he got away perfectly, took the bus up to about 6000 feet, looped it four times in succession, then put it into a spin, coming out beautifully. To give you an idea of what these buses are, I will simply say that at one time B. K.'s speed indicator registered 155 miles per hour! It was a splendid showing, and we are all waiting our turn, trusting we can do likewise and 'carry on.'

War requires of a man the display of more rugged qualities than a fine sensitiveness; and those rugged qualities Briggs Adams had, by direct inheritance. He was descended from Henry Adams, of Braintree, Massachusetts, the common ancestor of Samuel Adams and John Adams; and on his mother's side from the Wilson family of Virginia, of whom one member was killed fighting at Monmouth and another fell in the War of 1812. With such ancestry it is not surprising that Briggs Adams should have dedicated himself to the greatest of all struggles for human liberty. It is interesting and significant that his father and two brothers are in military service.

Most of the letters printed in this volume were written after he had enrolled in the Royal Flying Corps. It has, however, been thought wise to include a few letters written during his college period and while he was driving an ambulance in France, for the additional light that they shed upon his character and development.

His last letter was dated March 11, 1918. On March 14, a stormy and misty day, Briggs Adams was flying at the front, with a comrade of his squadron. The comrade missed him; and, descending, found him dead in his airplane in a field. It is not known whether he was brought down by an enemy projectile, or was the victim of an accident. All that is certain is that he was killed in active service while flying on the battle-front.

The appearance of a few of Briggs Adams's letters in the *Atlantic Monthly* for October, 1918, caused a widespread expression of deep interest. Thoughtful readers assigned to them a high place in the spiritual literature of the war. All that is noble and chivalrous in the American spirit is revealed in them; yet they were written by Lieutenant Adams with no thought of revealing anything to the world, but only to convey the warmth and encouragement of his spirit to those at home whom he dearly loved.

A.S.P.

Milton, Massachusetts
November 1, 1918

From Harvard

Westmorly Court, Cambridge, March, 1916.

Dear Mother and Father,—

If my examinations have been like the Sword of Damocles hanging over your heads, you can well imagine what it means to me to have that sword removed; for now I am absolutely clear of everything, and my path lies pretty straight ahead toward an A.B.; and along the side of that path I can see possibilities which may make the journey very pleasant. . . .

I am appreciating very much more what it means to have this opportunity for study here in college; I can almost *feel* myself growing and broadening from day to day,—not so much in technical knowledge, as in my capacity for appreciating things. I never could see, for instance, the use of learning about the life and character of an author, when it was his works which we read; but this week we have taken up the poet Pope in one of my courses, and having studied his life and realizing his acute sensitiveness, I can appreciate the state of mind which produced his great *Satires*.

Tonight I was reading the *Spectator* papers of Addison and Steele. I liked especially those about Sir Roger de Coverley. In high school we had to read and study them in a way which made them seem highly uninteresting; but tonight I seemed to get into the atmosphere of these delightful papers, and I fairly love the old knight for his simplicity and genuineness. He was constantly thinking of others, and yet, with all his Christian virtues, he had his own little foibles, such as napping in church, and sending his servants to waken others whom he had discovered asleep. His state of mind, so happily complacent, reminded me again and again of dear old Grandmother Adams as she always was, content with simple things, loving all and being loved by all who knew her, unquestioning in faith,—she really was a beautiful example.

The other night I took my violin out to play with H. M., and as we were playing Schubert's *Serenade* I recalled the picture of not so very long ago, when on a Sunday grandmother would be sitting in our library at home, fanning herself, and watching us sympathetically as we laughed and talked. Then Wilson and Beth would begin to play the *Serenade*, and her face would immediately light up with pleasure, she would draw her chair close to Wilson's, and sit there listening in perfect content. She had indeed no subtle or complex artistic appreciation of music, but loved it for its own sake, especially that *Serenade*.

I certainly enjoyed that evening with H. M. She is one of the few girls I know who, while being attractive, yet puts aside the feminine appeal, and you can enjoy her company quite impersonally. She plays well enough to read most of any accompaniments, and we played together all the old things, such as the *Swan Song*, the *Berceuse*, the *Serenade*, etc. I never played with better tone, and those old things, which seemed so uninteresting as I used to squeak through them in my old toneless days, when I was learning them, seemed now rarely beautiful to me, and I cannot begin to tell you how much I enjoyed that evening. I came back to college and slept like a log.

With much love from your devoted son.

First Views of War

Dear Father and Mother,—

The trip has been of the greatest interest so far because of its entire novelty. I had not realised a foreign country could be so foreign. On shipboard I noticed the change mostly in the cooking. Also the French are always shaking hands; when they meet in the morning, when they meet at lunch and when they go to bed.

The passengers held a sort of amateur concert two nights before we landed, for the benefit of the wounded soldiers. Among the various amateurs were two professionals, a *soprano* and a *tenor*, from the French Opera Company. They sang many of the familiar Victor records, and did very well so far as voices were concerned. The funny part was the way they pitched into it. The *soprano* would weep and laugh and work as hard as if she were before an audience of many thousands.

In closing, they sang the *Marseillaise* in a most dramatic manner. Most of the passengers were French, and they all stood up, and, holding their breaths tense, with eyes staring, they fairly drank in the words; and all joined in the chorus, shrieking, rather than singing it.

Among the seventy passengers, they raised something over twelve hundred *francs*, 125 of which I contributed; but not from my own pocket. They got the *tenor* and *soprano* to sign a program; and, as I had given them stories as my part of the show, they wished the job of auctioneering it off, on me. I surprised myself by finding my experience of farm auctions had not been forgotten. I strung an awful line of "bull." It went very slowly from 15 *francs* up. When it got up to 20 *francs* I saw it was doomed; so, pretending it was a great concession, I said that the one who would give 25 for it could have the program. (I wouldn't have given a quarter for it myself!) I noticed one Frenchman who had been bidding occasionally, so I sprung it on him as if he had said he would take it. And he was so surprised and sort of pleased to have the distinction that he said "Yes," and came across.

We had several hours in Bordeaux, which we spent driving around. As a foreign city it was very attractive, I thought; but it was strange to see stone buildings everywhere. The fare to Paris is something over forty *francs*. We came through free! It is pretty soft being an ambulance driver. One is not uncomfortable in plain clothes as in England, for here the army service is universal and it is only voluntary there. So if a man is in civilian clothes here they know he is either a foreigner or has some good reason; however, when in uniform, you are less conspicuous and you get half prices everywhere. Paris gets dark after sunset, but all the regular French places are going, except the opera and the Comédie Française.

The streets are crowded and busy, and everywhere you see women doing men's work. Conductors, street sweepers, clerks and the street venders, market-women and paper-sellers, singing their wares in some little tune of three and four notes, quite unlike the New York way. We were just about to go on the Bois before noon today, for we were told that was the time to see the classy stuff; but we had a call, and so had to remain nearby the Ambulance.

The dormitories were full, so about thirty of us fellows are staying in a vacant private house, which is referred to as the "*château*." When I heard I was to live in a *château*, I thought of the old days at the farm when Vincent was so amused by my remark, "*château*—big word!" From the street only a lot of little houses and high walls are to be seen. You pass through the gates from the porter's lodge, into a very lovely little court, very quiet, secluded and cool. The house is stripped now of all its furnishings, but it is easy to see that it was very luxurious.

The foreign part of it comes in again when it comes to water. There was not a bathroom in the house, so the Ambulance had one installed, three basins on the second floor, and three showers in the cellar, *for thirty to use all at once,* and just cold water at that!

There are six of us in a room that used to be a reception room on the ground floor, but my bed is near a window, so it is not bad. There are no hooks, no closets, no *chiffonier*, so you cannot unpack; and you have to have, your bags either under or on your bed. But all inconveniences are passed by with a shrug of the shoulder and the remark, "*C'est la guerre*."

We saw some terrible results of German warfare. I saw one man with only a slight wound, but whose nerves were so gone that he couldn't hold himself in a chair, but would literally shake himself off. Another fellow had both legs and arms gone, and his head all bandaged. Another whose face was burned to a charcoal. Eyes, nose, all gone, but living. One expects bullet wounds, or to lose a limb or two, even a head, if necessary, but to have a blackened misshapen *nothing* for a head and still live, makes you realise that not only is this the biggest but the most horrible war of all history.

I find only *thoughts* bother me. Even the odours in the Ambulance trains, which are awful, do not phase me. I am getting a lot of interesting experiences and even if I cannot go out to the front, I am close enough to hear the guns at night, and get first-hand accounts. It looks as if the big drive had really started, so we will be busy here for some time. But we have plenty of hands and will work in shifts, and so get on all right.

Much love to all.

American Ambulance, France, July 2, 1916.

Dear Linc,—

Much obliged for your nice steamer letter. I read it about half-way across. . . . All the Fords are out at the front, so I can drive a regular car after all. They do have some time at the front, believe me; I wish I could get out there. There is such a terrific noise, and so continuous, that it is almost like *quiet*.

One fellow was about fifty feet ahead of an ammunition wagon when a shell hit it and blew the whole thing up; killed the horses and driver, but the fellow driving the ambulance did not hear anything of it, until he was stopped and sent back.

All our cars are around Verdun, and after it is dark, they begin to work. They fall in line with the ammunition and food wagons and go along in pitch darkness and no lights. The Germans know exactly where the roads are now, so they can set their guns in a certain position and know they are hitting the road. They know the ammunition and reinforcements are coming up all night, and so they fire away and get a lot of them.

The Fords drive along as tight as they can. They cannot see the holes in the road that the shells make, so if they do not avoid them by instinct, they have to get lifted out by the constantly passing stream of soldiers; that is why they use Fords. They can pick them out of holes easier. If they manage to keep out of the holes they have to dodge the big wagons going the other way; horses going at full gallop, or big trucks tearing like mad. They cannot hear them coming because the noise is too great. Then to add to the *charm* of driving is the constant popping of shells. When they come back over the same road they find twenty or thirty new holes to fall into!

Any number of cars have been smashed, and fellows are getting nicked all the time, for they are more exposed than the men in the trenches. One fellow had a blow-out, so he got out to fix it. Just then a shell took off the seat he had left. Another driver was lying underneath his car fixing something. A shell hit it and knocked the car away and smashed it to bits, while he was left there lying on his back in the road with his hands reaching up holding a wrench, more surprised than you could imagine, and without a scratch.

Another fellow was famous for being the rottenest driver in that section. In one of the worst places he stalled his engine. While he was down cranking it, a shell went through his car killing one of the wounded fellows. The driver got his *Croix de Guerre* for bravery under fire! If he had been a decent driver he would have been out of the way and would not have got it.

"*This is a great life if you don't weaken.*"

Aeroplanes are as thick as flies about here. Just now I can see three playing tag, pretending one is a German and chasing it.

Study hard, Linc, so you can get up a class or two; for there may be a time like this when you would like to take a year off, but can't do it because you are getting too old, have to go to work, or get married!

Juilly, July 24, 1916.

Dear Family,—

Your "round-robin" of the first of July came last week and I as-

84

sure you it was much appreciated. I could see the big envelope standing addressed and stamped on the sitting room desk with *father's* letter in it, and hear his last word when leaving: "Be sure and get it off in time for the steamer."

It was very nice to get it and hear the news and see the snapshots, etc. But I hate to cause so much labor. As far as I am concerned I do not need any more letters here than when in Cambridge. For once here, the realisation of the distance separating us is lost, so hereafter only write when the spirit moves.

I have had a most perfect week here in the Ambulance. There are five squads of five cars each, and every week one squad calls out here to do what little work is necessary. It just happened we have not had a single train to meet, so we had nothing to do but enjoy ourselves. The town is just like a hundred other little French towns, nothing of interest in it except this old college, in which the hospital is temporarily located. The building is made of stone, the walls at least four feet thick at the base. It was begun in the twelfth century, and the college founded in the sixteenth. Jerome Bonaparte was one of the better-known graduates. It has a little park attached, with a pond, on which there are several swans swimming. It is the most peaceful, quiet place, full of suggestive atmosphere.

And the fellows in this squad are all very nice, and but one older than I, being in the thirties. The sergeant is an Englishman exempt from service for some physical trouble. He is a circus in himself. Every minute of the day he is saying or doing some ridiculously funny thing, and he has a very fine bass voice, by which ordinarily he earns his living. One evening we came upon a piano in one of the empty recitation rooms. One of the fellows sat down and began to play, and I happened to find a violin in good condition in the cupboard. The sergeant brought out some songs, and we spent a very enjoyable evening.

The food here is very much better than at the Ambulance at Neuilly. So to keep from getting stout I have to take long walks each day to some nearby town. Juilly is within a couple of miles of the farthest advance by the Germans on Paris in September, 1914, and the place where actual fighting took place is within easy walking distance. We hired a car the other day and went for quite a long ride, to and through the region of the Battle of the Marne, and it was very interesting. Hundreds of graves are lying in every direction according as the men fell, the Germans mixed in among the French, the former being marked only by a black stick, while the latter are marked by a wooden cross and a wreath or two. You would never believe one of the greatest battles of the world had been fought here; for everywhere rich crops of grain are growing, and nothing is prettier than the golden oats, among which are scattered red poppies and blue bachelor buttons, like kale in our oats at Hilltop Farms.

All the week we have had wonderful weather. First time It happened for a long stretch, so the week has been a treat and rest from the broken nights and the pressing work. The trouble with it is that we have so much of the unpleasant side of war, with none of the excitement of the front to make it worth while. Still I get a lot of anecdotes and tales from the fellows who come in from the front, so it is better than nothing. We return today and I shall now begin the French lessons I spoke of. It will give me something to work on at odd moments, and hearing French spoken on all sides, I ought to be able to pick up quite a lot before I leave.

Good food and walks each day this week have put me in prime condition, and it has been a relief to know that you can go to bed at night and can sleep till morning. In Neuilly you always feel agreeably surprised to find that it is morning, when you wake up, for so often it is night. *I am never going to be a fireman.*
The car we went out in the other day was hired. It had not been requisitioned because they thought it would not run. It looked as though it had been through the war, having but two cylinders, an old 1907 Renault with four gears. The fellow that owned it had half a dozen more scattered around his yard like it. They all seem to run, for I have seen him out in several different ones. One was a *one*-cylinder with everything so loose that it would flap all over the road from side to side as it ran. The old fellow would drive serenely along, leaning forward like Smalley in his Ford!

The other day we saw eleven aeroplanes in a bunch flying like a lot of swallows. You can never look up without seeing at least two or three flying around. If all America could move over and see a bit of this war, if only as little as I have seen, it would have a wonderful effect. It would make our people realise what a fearfully hateful crime it is, so that those who shout for war would quail and make themselves as small as possible, and the pacifists would get into uniforms and enter the trenches and fight to exterminate the rest of the Prussians from the earth. No one in America can begin to know what it is, no matter how much you read or have been told, it takes but a glance here to make the realisation almost insupportable, one just can't think. If the Germans could possibly ever be so *un*Germanised as to see it all in the true light, there would be a most terrific upheaval in Germany. France is using so much energy in the fight there is none left for the thought of the cost; they just go on paying, *paying*, and dying, *dying*; but no other of the belligerents is in it the way France is.

Much love and many thanks for the letters.

In the Air Service

R. F. C, Cadet Wing,
Long Branch, Ontario,
August 10, 1917.

Dear Mother,—

This is the first chance I have had to write, for we have been pretty busy. I got up here Wednesday morning and was all day taking the physical examinations and getting enrolled. I am now a British subject and will hold the commission when I get it till the end of the war. Ninety out of one hundred fellows in the corps are American. There is a company of Plattsburgers here studying aviation, and this morning the captain said we must "compete with the Americans in keeping our company streets cleaned up." It got quite a laugh when some one spoke up and said we couldn't "compete" with them, for we were all Americans.

The officers are all very attractive and treat us well. The whole place is well organised and no time is wasted on nonessentials. The camp is on the shore of Lake Ontario and we can look across and see the States dimly on the other side. The sun is hot in the middle of the day, but there is a good fresh breeze blowing all the time, so we keep cool and the nights are almost cold. We sleep in tents on comfortable cots with the wind blowing through. The food is very simple and might be worse prepared.

We shall probably be here a full week, maybe two or three, when we shall go back to Toronto for four weeks of studies. Then we go out to some nearby flying field for a couple of months' instruction in flying with a pilot. Then we go to the finishing field at Borden for flying alone; then we qualify for a

commission, but do not receive it until we get to England.
Much love to all.

Long Branch, Ontario, August 15, 1917.

Dear Father,—

They are working us very hard drilling, and the English drill is
tiring; they do not march in natural step but much faster, often
as high as 150 and not less than 140 per minute. Then on all the
turns there is a lot of stamping. The effect is very smart, but an
hour of it tires you out. We are in the British, not the Canadian
Army. When the branch was started in 1912, instead of being
made a minor branch of a minor branch, as ours is under the
Signal Corps, it was made the ranking regiment over all the
oldest and most famous English regiments, and now, as you
know, has a separate cabinet officer. In every way, by men and
officers, the R. F. C. is treated as the pet of the army. A couple
of fellows got "cold feet" the other day, before they had gone up
at all, just at the prospect; so they applied for discharge and were
given it. Some can't help being scared. Almost every one is, but
either they control the feeling or do not join in the first place.
I hope to be sent back to the University Monday. Or they may
keep us out here another week or more.

Long Branch, August 23, 1917.

Dear Dad,—

Today it is raining, so we do not have to drill for an hour before
breakfast as we generally do. That hour always seems the longest in the day because we are so empty. We get up at 5.30 and
don't breakfast until 8; today we are having only lectures, which
make a nice change.

Each afternoon a new lot of fellows come in, and at seven
o'clock, when the bugle blows for guard mount, we dress some
fellow up in an officer's uniform, get the new recruits out and
drill them for an hour or so; then we send them before a supposed medical officer who finds they have all sorts of diseases
for which they must be operated on, and they get scared to
death, for they are so green they do not see through it; then we
send them after so many yards of skirmish line, and "the key to
the camp," *et cetera*, finally marching them down to the lake for
a swim.

It certainly is getting like fall up here. The rumour is now pretty definite that all the aviation fields here in Canada will close September 25th, and we shall be sent to train for flying somewhere in the States, probably Texas.

R. F. C, Cadet Wing, South Residence,
University of Toronto, Canada, August 28.

Dear Mother,—

It is not harder here in the way of discipline as you said you feared it might be, for while they are more strict in the essentials and give heavier penalties for mistakes, etc., they treat the men in the R. F. C. exceptionally well. While still cadets we wear the officer's uniform, except for certain insignia on the shoulder strap and the belt; and, being considered as material for officers, we are supposed to be men and gentlemen and so do not have all the petty and aggravating rules and restrictions of privates in infantry. And the whole corps is the pride and pet of the army from top to bottom so they are given the best of everything. . . .

I make it a practice to think only in the present, getting what little I can out of it and taking whatever is handed out, without comment or question, and doing it in a sort of mechanical way. That is what they try to give you by discipline, so that when you are told to do something which you could never in the world do, ordinarily, you won't think anything about it and will have done it before you realise it. Most of the things that one thinks offhand are impossible are perfectly possible if one will just go ahead and make the effort that is necessary. . . .

Must stop now and write up some of my notes. Load of love to you.

South Residence, University of Toronto,
September 4, 1917.

Dear Father,—

We have a new commanding officer at the head of the school now, and, as always occurs when a new head comes in, there is a general and severe bracing up of all the departments. The last flight came through the course with a disgraceful record of 70% failure. Up here they make you take a course over again if you fail the first time. Consequently, we who come after have to suffer for it. They have cut down the time to be in barracks from 10.30 to 9.30 and actually prevent any going out weekday nights by holding a compulsory study hour from 7.30 to 9. As a result the fellows are chafing under the restraint. Unfortunately, they go about expressing their displeasure the wrong way, by doing all they can to make it hard for the non-coms. Inhibition is a great power in these times. It takes practice and strength, but it becomes easier with time, and it is the only way to keep going, and one has to keep going. To get up in the morning sooner than you want to; to go through a long day doing one thing after another that you don't want to do, trying to do it well, all for an end you hate the thought of; to be ordered about by nincompoops whom only the realisation that they are beneath resentment restrains you from kicking; to be punished for things you haven't done,—all this is bound to have some effect and in the end is going to have a good effect. Some fellows feel superior to an officer over them; but if a fellow is really superior, his superiority can stand the strain of dirty work and not be tarnished.

It is very easy in a short time knocking around with a bunch like this to pick out the real men. They are rather scarce, but when this business is over, while it may be a lot of those few men will be "pushing up the daisies," there will be a great many reborn out of a former shell. The great trouble with the men in the R. F. C. is that they haven't any sense of *esprit de* corps and the English have a great deal, because tradition of any sort means so much to them. Now the R. F. C. is the highest ranking regiment in all the English army, higher than all the old guard of hundreds of years' history, and it has existed only five years, but the best Canadians have all gone over before this and Americans, fellows of all sorts and characters, coming up here don't know the meaning of *esprit de corps*. It holds none for them. But after a while they will catch the spirit of the corps and take a real pride in their uniform which is distinct from any other in the army. . . .

Toronto, September 11.

Dearest Mother,—

Your letter of the eighth came tonight and it was great to hear from you and all the news from home. Some time has elapsed since I last wrote, but I have had a good reason. Just about a week ago the O. C. announced that the course from now on would be lengthened to six weeks, making the total including the Long Branch training, two months. And it meant we wouldn't get out of here till about the second week in October. Of course I am anxious to get to the real flying, so I wrote a letter to the chief instructor stating the work I had done and requesting that I be allowed to take my exams with the course ahead of ours, who took them yesterday and today. It was granted, so I had to begin and work under forced draft to get my notebook finished and the ground covered and reviewed. I have taken the exams and think that I passed all. But I cannot be sure, because some of them were rather tricky. I will hear definitely in three or four days. It will be fine if I did. ... I will have a good start on the other fellows, and afterward, a vacation will be more satisfactory, for I shall have accomplished some real flying. Then I will be able to tell you all about it, and when people ask me, "Have you been up yet?" I can answer nonchalantly that I have, with a true English air of boredom! There are some very amusing bored Englishmen among our instructors and officers.

We were all put on C. B. (confined to barracks) last week till they found out who the fellows were who had roughed up one of the non-coms, one night. Of course it was grating on the fellows who had nothing to do with it to have to stay in barracks on Saturday and Sunday, so about thirty just walked out. As a result several of them were dishonourably discharged, and the remainder were sent back to Long Branch for four weeks. I certainly was glad that I stuck to the rules. In army life there are lots of rules in every direction that you turn, but I realize the truth of something Dr. Bradford said many years ago, that the freest man was the one who obeyed the laws most strictly. A lot of fellows here use up a great amount of time devising methods to get round the rules which, if they obeyed, would give them more time to do what they want, and invariably in the end they get caught up for it. Whereas the man who makes a habit of obeying the rules soon forgets that there are any and is not conscious of any restraint. You see I am becoming disciplined a little, and I hope in the right way; not the German method of crushing the spirit of resistance, but the Anglo-Saxon way of making the individuals discipline themselves for the good of all.

You know that expression "carry on" is used by officers when they come into a room, when of course every one has to stop whatever he is doing and spring to attention. You hear them say that and "as you were" more than anything else.

I am feeling in perfect health, as the food is excellent here and the hours regular, and of course with a healthy body I cannot help feeling fine mentally.

Lots of love for you.

Squadron 85, Camp Rathbun.
Deseronto, Ontario, September 15.

Dear Mother,—

Well, I got by, and have been shipped out here about 140 miles from Toronto. Less than half of the course, with whom we three Course Twelve fellows took our exams, passed. So it is very gratifying to have done so, as it means several weeks' gain.

This camp certainly is fine. Here we are more like officers than heretofore, we have an extra fine mess, comfortable quarters, and in every way the atmosphere is different. This is just a line to let you know how I came out and my present address. I will write you more when I have been up, which will be on the first good day.

Squadron 85, Camp Rathbun,
Deseronto, Ontario, September 15, 1917.

Dear Father,—

. . . Deseronto is a little country town on the north bank of the St. Lawrence about half way between Toronto and Montreal. It is quite a pretty country and there is a fine level aerodrome to work on. The quarters are very comfortable. There is quite a difference in the attitude here. We seem to be one step further toward being officers and not such low-down privates as we were at Toronto.

Well, this is the beginning of another step in the progression. The first was at Long Branch where we were supposed to get discipline. The next at the Elementary Training Wing, and last at the Higher Training Wing.

Tomorrow I go up for my "joy" ride. It certainly will be interesting, and just as soon as I show the ability, I will do the solo work, which I have to do for ten hours. If the weather is good some fellows get in their ten hours in a week. So in all I might not be away more than three or four months. It certainly is gratifying to have passed out of the school ahead of time.

Now comes the real thing, and it will be much more fun. I will write soon and tell you how I take to the air and what it is like.

The First Flying

Squadron 85, Camp Rathbun,
Deseronto, Ontario, September 18, 1917.

Dear Father and Mother,—

Smashes are of hourly occurrence on the aerodrome, but they all occur either in landing or getting off, so there is no fall, and the men get out without a scratch every time. Yesterday the fellow in the next bunk to mine went right over upside down and crawled out from underneath with nothing more than a *bump on his nose!* The machine was taken in and before night it was out and being used again. It is remarkable the way they can be banged round and stand it. Every time a fellow crashes, he has so much more confidence; for he sees that he cannot be hurt. You see, you have a belt to hold you in and so cannot be thrown out and break your neck. The best flyer is seldom the one who has never had a crash. Machines alight in very peculiar positions, and I expect to be able to get some very interesting pictures to show you when I come home. The closer I get to flying the less I am afraid of it, for you see it is a matter of science and common sense and not some mysterious power. And the dubs that get away with it are in themselves sufficient to remove all trepidation.

When called for early morning flying, as I was this morning, you get up at 4.30 and have to be down at the hangars at 5.30, after getting some coffee and sandwiches. This morning I had my "joy" ride. That is what they call the first ride. I sat in the front seat and was taken up about a thousand feet and after a few minutes brought back to the aerodrome. The getting off is the most exciting part, as the speed seems great, and any moment the machine seems as if it might take a notion to tip over on its nose. But soon the bumps grow less and after a hundred yards or less they cease entirely and you are clear of the ground.

Then the ground slips rapidly away beneath you and the sense of speed is lost. I never saw anything more beautiful than the country this morning from up there. You could see for miles, and everything stood out distinct, but absolutely flat. The fields were laid out like a pattern in soft plush, varying from the golden yellow of the ripe grain fields to green of grass and brown of ploughed land. When gliding back to earth the gliding angle seems very steep, but not enough to trouble your stomach. As you approach closer to the ground, you are conscious once more of the speed. Soon you are skimming over it only a few feet above, and gradually settle down with a few bumps and come to a stop.

Tomorrow I go up again "dual," but am given the controls and fly in a straight line. The next day I take a slight curve, increasing it from day to day till the instructor feels certain that I am capable of handling the machine alone. Then I go up "solo" and can do mostly as I please. If I have good luck and too many of the machines are not smashed, I should be "soloing" by the end of the week.

Lots of love to all.

Squadron 85, Camp Rathbun,
Deseronto, Ontario, September 20.

Dear Father,—

I have had about an hour in the air now and I no longer feel any nervousness or confusion as at first. This forenoon I went up with the instructor for thirty-five minutes and took all the controls after we had got up a couple of thousand feet and ran the machine straight and round some curves, and when we came down he said that I did very well indeed for the first time at the controls. The previous times I have just ridden with my hands on the controls lightly to get the feel of it. I think I shall get onto it quite quickly and by the first of next week be "soloing," if we have good luck and no more of the machines are smashed. Each flight has five machines, but we only have two in commission at present. But they get them fixed up very quickly, and a lot of fellows are finishing up, so we will get in a lot of instruction, as there are only two of us in my flight that are not "soloing."

Dear Mother,—

Just a line before going to bed to let you know that I am getting along well. I have now had 150 minutes and can handle the machine with great confidence in the air. The instructor is going to start me on landings tomorrow. They are really the only difficult thing to get onto in flying and they are soon mastered. I think the end of next week will see me about finished here. Then we go to Camp Borden till it is time to go to Texas.

Today was one of those perfect late September days. We went up about 3 this afternoon till we got an elevation of slightly less than five thousand feet. You could see miles and miles in every direction. From any altitude above a thousand you no longer see any contours. The country looks like a vast circular flat, slightly concave, the circle of the horizon being highest. That is what you guide by in keeping the machine level. Looking below I steered by the roads, which looked like very thin white ribbons.

I discovered that the water which I thought was the St. Lawrence was only a long inlet on Lake Ontario. The trees, which are rapidly becoming coloured with the autumn tints look like small round spots of colour flat on the ground. When the air is clear this way it is usually bumpy; that is, there are numerous up-and-down currents as well as horizontal ones caused by the air rising or falling over spots on the ground which absorb more heat than others and so heat up the air above them. These bumps give a delightful irregularity to the flight. When it is calm, straight flying becomes boring, but bumps make you keep awake. You sail along smoothly and all of a sudden the machine drops away like an elevator going down, and you reach up to get your stomach which feels as if you had left it several feet above! Then you hit an up-current and the machine comes up and spanks you a good one, and you rise up anywhere from ten to fifty feet; then all is smooth as before. Those bumps do not cause any tendency to seasickness, but on the contrary are very exhilarating.

The air is cold and very bracing, and when you come down, you feel as if you had taken a tonic. Coming down after being up at an even altitude for some time seems somewhat as if you were stepping off a plateau like the floating island that Swift tells about in *Gulliver's Travels*. The first time I took a glide my stomach came up in my throat with a thump, for the gliding angle is pretty steep, but now it seems like the best part.

There was a collision in the air today, but it was only about fifty feet from the ground and as usual no one was even scratched. Yesterday a machine was smashed in a landing so that there seemed to be little left of it but the engine, and this morning when we came down it was rolled out ready to fly. They certainly do things quickly and efficiently here. I am telling you about the smashes which occur because they are so frequent and so harmless that I want you to see how little real danger there is in the training. Our emblem is a cat painted on the side of the machine—nine lives. After each smash they put a white dot on its tail. Some of the cats have five and six dots, and the machine is as good as new. They take great pains to see that it is as good as new and will tear down a whole machine and reassemble it for the slightest doubt; there is no such thing as flying unsafe and condemned machines here.

Squadron 85, Camp Rathbun,
Deseronto, Ontario, September 23, 1917.

Dearest Mother,—

...We had to get up this morning as usual, though it is Sunday. It was still dark with the stars shining when I went over to get my coffee and sandwiches, and I was in the air before the sun came up. After the war, machines will be very cheap because of the big production which the war is causing, so I will have one and take you up some early morning to see the wonder of a sunrise above the clouds. It is indescribable. I had not thought when choosing this branch that besides the cleanliness and other attractive features there was such marvellous beauty connected with it. Even war cannot look horrible from up there. And there is such a wonderful feeling of exultation over the universe; to fly along at a high elevation where there are no bumps, the machine seemingly suspended by an invisible thread which gently gives and sways as you pass through different currents of air; driving a machine which responds like a muscle of your own body to the slightest thought of the brain. "What is that town like over there to the left?"—already before you have scarcely seen it the machine has turned and is going closer. "What is that queer-looking object below?"—at once the engine is shut off and you are gliding down like a bolt one, two, three thousand feet till you can make it out. "I wonder how it is up there above that cloud?"—up the machine goes steadily climbing like a willing slave to execute your every whim.

You and all the family are going to ride with me after the war, for after the first time you will not have a moment's nervousness. It seems twice as secure and just as natural as sitting in a car. . . .

Camp Borden, Ontario, October 5, 1917.

Dearest Mother,—

The weather has been very unsettled since coming here, so flying has been in bunches. I have only made about eight flights, totalling six hours, so I am afraid I won't be able to make the next gunnery course. However, it doesn't matter a great deal, for I can go along slowly and it won't be long after I get to England before I finish. I should like to have received my commission before going over, but it makes no difference in the end.

Every day I wish you could look in on the aerodrome, because it would remove your nervousness. The more you learn about flying and the more familiar you become with it, the more understandable and reasonable it seems. For example, what I am working on now is "vertical banks." That is, taking a corner so sharp that you turn your wings up sideways, vertical to the ground. To watch from the ground, it seems as if the machine must sideslip down like a bullet, and yet the centrifugal force of the turn holds it as securely in place in the air as if the air were a solid substance like a banked-up corner on a race-track.

Also, I am working on spiral glides. Heretofore, when about to land, I would get way off so that I could glide in a straight line down. Now I can be right over a field I wish to land on and spiral down from any altitude on to it. This is a valuable acquisition, because in case of engine failure I can be more sure of landing where I want to. These things aren't stunts at all—they are merely elementals, and even the stunts aren't really stunts, for there is a definite place to put your controls, a definite way to change them, and when you place them so, the machine will go through the movements desired. . . .

Yesterday, two machines collided 600 feet above ground—one only had its propeller broken, and glided down easily on the aerodrome. The other was completely cut in half and fell down straight, nose first, and half buried itself in the ground; but before landing it crashed into a tree. The pilot was thrown out and had his fall broken, so that he got up, dusted off his clothes and strolled back to the aerodrome literally without a scratch. Today, as is the case every day, there were four crashes, all outside the aerodrome, and not a soul hurt. Yet one of the mechanics, cranking a propeller, had his leg broken when the engine kicked back. So flying is safer than cranking, you see.

Today I got in a couple of hours of formation flying. We start out six machines and climb up to a stated altitude over a certain rendezvous point; then form up in a V, like a flock of wild geese. It is harder than flying alone, for you have to keep the formation on turns. This means the outside machines have to nose down a bit to get additional speed and the inside machines throttle down and nose up. It is very good practice; now all work at the front—reconnaissance, flights, bombing raids, fighting—is done in squadron formation. . . . This is to prevent one machine as heretofore from falling in with a lot of Hun machines and being surrounded and brought down. Now it is a court-martial offence to cross the line alone, except for certain individuals like Major Bishop, who has brought down about forty. . . .

This evening the clouds were remarkably low—500 feet—and several of the machines got lost in different parts of the country round about. They came down on some field and telephoned in that they would come back in the morning.

I was up before lunch and got caught in a very heavy rain-shower. Had no windshield on the machine I was driving, and the big drops of rain hitting my face at 60 miles an hour stung like bees. When I got in, the edge of the hard oak propeller was rasped, as if a big rough file had been rubbed over it; but when you consider the propeller tip is travelling round 600 feet per second, it isn't surprising. They put a new one on, for the slightest blemish destroys the balance, which must be perfect, since revolving at such a high speed, it would gradually vibrate till it broke itself up. The aeroplanes are truly wonderfully made things,—like a Swiss watch, and when you see the way they get banged around, it shows the remarkable workmanship that is put into them.

This letter is mostly all "shop," but there is little else to talk about. I am learning more and gaining confidence by large doses every day. I don't even tighten up when making landings now, and with high winds, gusty and all, I certainly have had some bumpy rides.

Deep love.

Camp Borden, October 6, 1917.

Dear Mother and Father,—

The weather remains unsettled,—windy and bitterly cold,— so we are working under difficulties. I made three flights this morning, of about an hour each. The clouds were low, so I had a lot of valuable practice going through them. They are veritable whirlpools of criss-cross currents. . . . I worked in them about an hour, till I felt fairly confident. . . . When I came down, my machine was glazed with ice from the condensed vapour freezing. I never was so cold, in spite of two sweaters, coat and heavy lined leather overcoat. But a 60-mile wind below freezing-point is bound to get through anything. I honestly don't see how they can keep this place going a month longer, as they intend to, the days are getting so short and the weather so bad. I would rather have been spanked than go up again after my second trip, but I had to go just the same.

Before breakfast I went up to about 5000 feet, where there wasn't a bump,—about 1000 feet above the clouds,—and I sailed along for an hour watching a glorious sunrise. The clouds looked so fleecy white, all billows and projections; and an occasional one towered up like an iceberg. It made me feel as if I might be standing at the North Pole on a snow-covered ice floe. The place seemed to have the stillness of the North Pole; not a sound, nothing stirring the least bit. I couldn't see the ground, so the illusion was complete, particularly the cold,—there was no illusion about that. I spoke of the stillness, which is a fact. For the noise of the engine is smoothed into a sort of roar by the wind, and this roar being absolutely constant, you cease to notice it after a time, and it becomes a state; thus absolutely whispering silence is there in effect. But let that engine miss or slow down the least bit, and at once you hear it, just as when you hear a clock stop which you haven't noticed ticking.

I went way up then, because I wanted to try some vertical banks, and whenever trying anything new, the higher you are, the safer, for it gives you more time to recover in case of trouble. A fellow was killed here today because he tried a stunt when only a few hundred feet over the ground; whereas another fellow yesterday tried the same stunt, missed it the same way, and went into a nose-dive, but after 1500 feet was able to get out of it. A little time and space is all that is necessary to recover from any imaginable position. So you see I am very cautious, and I wasn't even trying anything very difficult.

The nearest example to a vertical bank that I can think of is what you may have seen at some vaudeville or circus some time, where a man gets inside of a huge barrel-shaped affair made of slats and rides a bicycle round in it. As he gains in speed he can move farther and farther up the sides till he is perpendicular to them. Ordinarily you take an easy bank or something less than 45. But when you bank steeper, you have to use your elevator as rudder and rudder as elevator. The transition came more naturally than I expected it would. But the way that nose swept round the horizon was a caution. You know, sighting along the top of the engine-cover to the radiator, you always keep your level by the horizon line. That is why when in a cloud you no longer can be sure she is longitudinally level. You can always see a lateral change in the machine itself.

I tried several vertical banks on each side till I was sure I had the idea. Now I have three things I didn't have when I came up, all of the utmost value: the spiral glide, which makes a safe landing possible in case of engine failure; confidence in clouds, which often have to be traversed; and a vertical bank, of great value in avoiding a collision. . . . That vertical bank will turn you about in a circle that must be no greater than 100 feet in diameter; and when you consider that you are travelling in one direction over 60 miles an hour, and turn about and go in the opposite direction in that small radius, it is *some* turning. . . . . It took me quite a while to start the first vertical bank, for, unlike making the first landing, you didn't have to make this. Something kept urging, "Oh, go in; wait till another time; no one will ever know the difference." And then, "Well, you have got to do it some time or go down and be a mechanic." So do it I did, and the doing was many times easier than the determining. And each thing I do will make it easier to do the next, like a habit; also each accomplishment gives such a gain in confidence.

Dear Father and Mother,—

In spite of the weather I am progressing steadily, and, as I wrote Beth yesterday, expect, with good luck, to be coming home inside of three weeks for my final leave before going overseas.

I heard a little inside dope today that first we go to Scotland for the aerial gunnery course which I won't get here. That takes about three weeks, then we are sent to France to an aerodrome where we learn to fly the actual machines used, which, while controlled similarly, are a bit different in actual flying because of their high speed. After that, we return to England for final training, where we pass certain tests and do a bit of instructing; then we are sent to the front as we are needed. So you see the preliminary trip to France will make an easy breaking in for the final trip, and if I can continue to do the work, whatever it is, not exceptionally, but creditably, it will be sufficient satisfaction to you as well as myself; and if anything happens to me, it wouldn't matter. It isn't *when*, but *how*. A good "how" can go a long way toward making up for a "when" for all concerned, and of course this is looking at the extreme, which need not occur necessarily.

There is so much to do each day that it gives one a gratifying sense of progressing constantly. There are five so-called ground tests having to do with wireless and miniature artillery observation. I have been taking mine at odd moments when weather was bad for flying, and today passed the last two off somewhat ahead of those who came in the same day with me; also today took my first though easiest flying test—the altitude test. That is to climb up 8000 feet and glide all the way down in one stretch with the engine shut off, and at last touch in a circle 100 feet in diameter on landing. I started out for an hour's formation flying, but they took so long to get the engine started that the formation had gone, so I went up to stow away some time.

After a while I noticed the clouds were much more broken up, so I decided I might as well practice the altitude test and climbed up. It was terribly cold up there; then I shut off and came down the mile and two-thirds in about five minutes. It was a decided strain on the ears, for ordinarily you level out for a while every few thousand feet to let them become adjusted, but in this test you can't put the engine on at all. I came down and not only touched the circle, but stopped dead right in the middle of it, so I taxied in and reported to the officer in charge and he gave me credit for it. The wind was very high today—at times 40 miles an hour—and I am getting so I can handle the machine with perfect assurance in all kinds of weather conditions.

The next test is to go up 13,000 feet and make two eights between two points and spiral down as before with engine off and stop in the circle. This must be done twice. The glide is easy, for my ears are used to small continuous glides like that. The only hard part is to stop in the circle. It takes a lot of practice and judgment, for you have to consider the strength of the wind and you are apt either to come short or roll through and beyond. In an ordinary landing on the aerodrome if you haven't enough height to reach the field on a glide, you can give her the gun and level off for a while. But this is not merely landing on the field, but coming to a stop in what is practically a pretty small point.

It is a valuable accomplishment, for in case of a forced landing on a small field, you can make sure of doing it all right. After a cross-country flight to Toronto, which is very easy, and a total of thirty-five hours,—I now have twenty-two,—I am transferred to the Wireless Squadron, where I carry out an actual artillery observation, reading the ground signals—strips of white cloth and certain figures meaning code messages. I wireless down my observation of the shell-bursts; also I do some photographing of certain specified points. That is hard, for you have to sight the camera and fly the machine at the same time, but I notice already that I fly it a great deal by feeling.

Camp Borden, Ontario, October 10, 1917.
Dear Father and Mother,—
Today I got off the second flying test after a couple of tries, so now all I have is about two hours' more formation flying and a cross-country, but I shall delay them until the end of the week if I can stall off, for I want to soak away a lot of time to my credit. As soon as you have done them, they transfer you to the Wire-

less Squadron where you don't get much time in, and the closer to fifty hours I have here, the sooner I will get my commission on the other side. I have now about twenty-six.

This is really the first pleasant day we have had since I came up here. It wasn't so raw and cold, and much less wind, though it changed about constantly in direction, so that once I nearly had a crash, for coming down the way I took off into the wind; I saw by the excessive speed as I came close to the ground that I was going right with the wind, but I gave her the gun before it was too late and came down again in the opposite direction.

One of the fellows I like best up here—a fellow from Elizabeth—was trying the same test as I. He glided down, but as he came close to the ground saw that he wasn't going to even reach the aerodrome, so he gave her the gun, but the engine wouldn't pick up. It just coughed and sputtered, so he had to keep on coming down and crashed into a tree. The machine was a total wreck, but he got out with only a gashed lip, and jolt.

You see, the safety belt holds you in the machine so when it crashes you can't be thrown out and hurt, and the crumpling up serves to check the fall, and, being back of the planes of engine, you aren't likely to be hurt at all, except for a bump on the nose from the cowling. Now you are worrying, saying, Suppose your engine hadn't picked up; but if it hadn't I was right over the aerodrome, so it would not have mattered. I always fly within gliding distance of the aerodrome, because these engines are used so constantly they are none too reliable; but if you are up a mile, that means you can be 5 or 6 miles away and have a safe margin for gliding in, and a circle with a 10-mile diameter means a 30-mile circuit, so it leaves quite sufficient area for flying around.

There was a half-inch of ice in puddles this morning, after a clear, cold night. I was just thinking today how very civilized the world had become in spite of the fact that war still exists. All my life I have taken mattresses, hot water, sheets, pillows, etc., as such absolutely matter-of-course things; and now sleeping in blankets out in the cold, with no sheets, mattress or pillow, shaving in cold water,—it really isn't so bad after all, but it does make you realise what civilization has done for physical comfort and convenience by supplying the things which are not at all necessary to existence, but do add a tremendous amount of comfort.

I am looking forward immensely to my leave spent in a warm house with all its accessories. It won't be long now, I am pretty sure—less than three weeks. With a heart full of love,

Camp Borden, October 14, 1917.

Dearest Mother,—

Now, I want to tell you something which I haven't up to this time, because I wanted to save you needless anxiety. It can't make you anxious now, for I have completed it, and shall do no more stunts. I did not expect to do any when I first came here, but finally decided I must, for I was afraid to. The fellow who had done them seemed to have no more to him than I have, and I am determined to be as good as any and better than most, for only so can I expect much chance of coming back. The dubs and boneheads get picked off quickly, and likewise those who lack the nerve to do something and hesitate an instant too late in an emergency. So you see I had to get rid of every atom of fear and gain this quality which a few others seemed to have. It isn't dare-deviltry or rashness; before going up I had the mechanic look at the machine and give it a thorough inspection so that I could be sure it would not give way. Then I talked with the officer and found out exactly what to do.

First I tried a loop, and that is the easiest of all stunts, requiring a simple gain in speed by nosing down slightly and then pulling straight up until she gets up over. It is a wonderful sensation to feel the machine rise up and up on its graceful curve as if some giant hand were tossing it; then the swoop down and out onto the level. I tried several until I lost all sense of confusion and was perfectly aware where I was in any position. It is ten times easier to do than the vertical bank, for that requires a reversal of the controls and use of all three. In the loop there is only one simple straight back, the other two being neutral. Next time I went up I tried a stall and tail-slide. That is much the same as a loop, only having less speed. You merely go up until the machine is vertical up and down. There you lose headway, shutting off the engine, and slide tail-first for the ground.

And as you begin to move, the air gets under the tail and begins to lift it. The weight of the engine drops the nose and you come out in a simple glide. It is easier even than the loop. I did it second because the sensation was rather strong.

Then we had a couple of bad days until today. Meanwhile, I was figuring. I asked myself, What is the worst possible sensation I can get. I decided it would be the tail-slide upside down, so I worked out a way that I could do it. Starting out at a simple stall, I went slightly past top vertical; then pushed the elevator clear forward, which allowed the air when dropping to hit the top side of the tail instead of the bottom as in the ordinary tail-slide. This got the desired motion—tail-sliding upside down; but very quickly the tail was lifted further, the engine dropping, and the machine completed the backward somersault, coming out as usual in the simple nose-down glide, when I pulled up level. Next I tried the so-called Immelman turn, where you nose up nearly vertical, slide down sideways and pull up out of the nose-glide, going in the opposite direction. It is a turn invented by Immelman and is the shortest possible way of going in the opposite direction,—far quicker than a vertical bank turn and a most effective manoeuvre for an aerial fighter.

Having done now all possible stunts that the Curtis machine is capable of and in addition invented a stunt of my own, I started in and just threw the machine around this way and that, letting it fall sideways, backwards, every way, chucking the controls this way, criss-crossing them, letting them go entirely; always the weight of the engine would swing her down and straighten out in a simple nose-glide, from which it is easy to pull out level. Now I feel that I have banished every single atom of fear of this new element, air. I feel quite gratified that I have done so, for now no matter what happens I can't feel afraid and get rattled. Many fellows have been killed by being thrown accidentally in a bad position and getting scared and rattled. I can't be killed in flying now. You see, when I get to fighting, not having to think of my machine, I can concentrate every attention on the fighting and so bring down an adversary.

There are only a dozen out of the whole camp, exclusive of officers, who have done even the simplest stunts, and my rather novel stunt has caused quite a little interest, which is of course fun for me. Of course it has often been done before in different machines, but it is a new one for this camp.

Now I have accomplished my purpose, I shall do no more until we get over to the other side where the machines are built and

adapted for such things.
Ever so much love.

Camp Borden, October 15.

Dear Mother and Father,—

. . . It seems quite definite now that we go to Texas for the aerial gunnery course which takes three weeks. Probably on account of the transfer it will consume nearer four, but after it I will receive my commission and have it before going over, so this leave which I hope I can get in about the last five or six days of the month will not be a final one. For that reason I would rather not have you plan any festivities at this time, but let them come in the final leave a few weeks later when I have the shoulder-straps, stars and wings. That will be something worth while celebrating, for, believe me, that is a commission earned, if anything is. Let this present leave be a nice pleasant family visit. Of course I will enjoy a theatre and a concert or two particularly.

I have missed music like a food, for I got such a great deal of it last year after I left college that I felt a decided gap.

When I was finally able to secure a machine this morning, I stayed up two hours, which is a safe margin on the gasoline supply, in order to get in all the time I could while I had a machine. The wind was pretty strong when I left the ground, and it increased until it finally equalled the speed of the machine—over 60 miles per hour; and flying into it I stayed stationary over the same point on the ground, so to divert myself I nosed up and climbed to 11,000 feet, which is slightly over two miles. It seemed about the same there as at a mile, except objects were somewhat smaller. I intended seeing how high the bus would climb, but I got so cold I couldn't stand it any longer, so glided down to about 3000 feet.

There the wind was very dusty, and clouds a short distance above inclined to make it bumpier than I have ever experienced it so far, and yet I am so used to flying now that I can do it entirely by feeling and no longer have to think about it. So I flew for nearly an hour, looking down on the ground and thinking about home and after the war. That is a welcome improvement, for I used to get very bored doing nothing for two hours but sit there and concentrate on the machine. Finally the two hours were up, and I circled over the aerodrome and noticed there was another machine on it and looking around could not see one in the air where usually you could see at least twenty or thirty. So I realized the wind must be even stronger than I thought and decided I had better get down. I nosed down very steeply, the engine partly on, and when I touched the ground the machine didn't roll more than 20 feet. If it were not for the trees I could easily have landed on our little back terrace at "Irvingcroft."

There were a lot of mechanics out all over the aerodrome, who grabbed the machine, but the minute I turned sideways, the wind nearly turned me up on one wing. Two or three fellows had crashed coming in shortly before me, so I was very pleased to foil all their expectations and get away with it all right, but flying was washed out for the rest of the day, and yet today was the most perfect we have had, not considering flying value.

I fear this letter is rather verbose, yet I couldn't experience such a day without being affected by it and trying to give you as much a share of it as my powers of expression would permit. If you can really picture it rather than just realize it is something you missed and so envy me for it, I shall feel very happy; but I am determined that you shall experience it at first hand some time.

Among the Clouds

Dear Mother,—

This afternoon the sky was full of those great broken masses of thick puffy white clouds with sky appearing so clear and deep blue between them. I climbed up between some until I was on top a thousand feet, then I flew along for an hour or more with the wheels just touching their upper surface. I could almost imagine they were turning. It seemed like riding in a mythical chariot of the gods, racing along this vast infinitely white field stretching off endlessly in every direction. The clear open sky above veritably is heaven as we imagined it in childhood. Occasionally I would pass over an opening so I could look down and get my location direction, but except for these occasional breaks the world was completely shut out. The celestial illusion was perfect, and it was hard to come away from it—really quite a tug.

Then came the glide down—a wonderful sensation to pass through the air with engine shut off so that you really seemed to be floating, or rather swimming like a fish in water, making great sweeping spiral curves. . . . Sometimes I would drop and tear through the air like a meteor at 150 miles an hour, with the wires shrieking with the wind, then nose up again and slow down. Oh! I wish so much you could have been with me on that ride, for you would have enjoyed it. It was so beautiful, and to get away above the world that way—outside of it in a heaven of absolutely unmarred beauty! . . . You seem to expand with it—where there is no measure there are no bonds. . . .

I went up again just before sunset and remained until the sun had gone down. I flew toward the sunset until I was actually in those frail mists of vapour which assume such exquisite colours. When seen from the ground they seem to be colon painted on the plane surface of the sky. Up there the different strata of colour and irregular bits of cloud seem to stand out in relief like the figures in a picture seen through a stereoscope. Flying close to one of these wisps so intangible in substance and yet so clothed in colour, I felt the impulse to put out my hand and touch it, touch and feel colour in its substanceless essence. Tenderest love.

Camp Borden, October 19, 1917.

Dear Mother,—

We are living out in tents now—the barracks are reserved for the present aerial gunnery fellows. It certainly is disagreeable out here most of the time—the weather is below freezing-point, and so damp!

I am in such good health I can't take cold, but it is no fun. It rained all last night, and my tent was leaking in a dozen different places. It certainly is good for one, if unpleasant, to get out of bed at 5 in the morning while it is still pitch black, and dress, put on shoes stiff with cold with fingers that ache like teeth, stumble down to the hangars and go up in the air, a 60-mile gale blowing, below freezing, and stick it out for two hours at a stretch. I never have been so cold so consistently and so continually before. For while you can bundle up, your clothes are icy when you put them on, and in the air your feet soon get absolutely numb. Sometimes when I come down I cannot walk. . . .

Yesterday I was sent up to read some ground signs. That is a shutter arrangement which is open and shut revealing white, and done in the time of dots and dashes of the regular telegraphic code. You fly over it and read the message. This is the work of the next squadron, but I was able to get permission to do it ahead of time. You have to get fifteen words in all. I got ten the first trip, which is doing well; but the wind was in my favour, for by throttling down till the machine just had flying speed to support it, I could stay directly over the same spot the whole time and never once had to look at the machine, keeping my eyes constantly on the ground, for I can drive entirely by feeling now without any thought of the machine. I would get a word, then write it down on the tablet on my knee, and look down again for the next one; so I have these ten to my credit and only need to get five more.

I was able to get a very good idea of fighting the other day. When we get into the aerial gunnery course, they send up two machines and one has a camera instead of a gun, with regular gun sights. They manoeuvre about—the one trying to avoid the other, who pulls the trigger and takes the picture when he has him in line. Two of us were sent up in ordinary machines to get some preliminary practice in manoeuvring. The O. C. said go up and fly around on each other's tails, but keep a couple of hundred yards apart. The other fellow was a good flyer, so we mixed it up, sailing and darting around, dodging and diving, often passing within fifty feet. There was no danger of our colliding, however, for we had very definite signals. . . .

We battled for about an hour in such a realistic manner that from the ground we had them all holding their breath; at a distance you cannot see the actual distance between the machines. When we came down the O. C. said, "That was very good." My machine was about five miles an hour faster and yet this slight advantage enabled me to fly circles around the other. I could shake him off my tail any time I pleased and keep him constantly in bead of my supposed gun, and that is what fighting depends largely on.

Camp Borden, October 23, 1917.

Dearest Mother,—

. . . I have felt when I was above there with the world shut out that I might meet Carol, for it does not seem as though I were in this life at all. The beauty and unreality and the absolute aloneness are so totally different from any known experience in all the world's history that you cannot feel yourself. It seems as if it was just your spirit. The grotesque fanciful shapes of cloud projections as you wind in and out among them are so incomparably white, the air is so cold and so devoid of dust and moist particles, that it seems as if there were no air at all. With the illusion of absolute, awful stillness, little wonder that I could feel that I might come upon her on the other side of the next cloud. . . .

The Figure of War

Camp Borden, October 24, 1917.

Mother Dear,—

I feel no bitterness against the Huns as individuals or as a race. It is war that I hate, and war that I am willing to give all to end as permanently as possible, for it isn't the men that war kills, it is the mother's heart which it destroys, that makes it hateful to me. War personified should not be the figure of death on a body-strewn battlefield, as it so often is. It should be pictured as a loathsome male striking a woman from behind—a woman with arms tied, but eyes wide open. To kill that figure because it has struck my own mother—that is why I am exerting myself and all the will in my being to accomplish. It hurts me so to think of the ever-growing hopelessness that a mother has to bear. The impotency to do anything—just sit and wait, wait, wait.

It is so immeasurably harder than to go out and risk death, or meet it, as we can. . . . To me it seems like a great final examination in college for a degree *summa vita in mortem*, and it challenges the best in me—spurs me on to dig down for every last reserve of energy, strength and thought. As I said in my letter to Dr. Mills,—a thought suggested by Dr. Black,—*"Death is the greatest event in life,"* and it is seldom that anything is made of it. What a privilege then to be able to meet it in a manner suitable to its greatness! Once in your life to have met a crisis which required the use of every last latent capacity! It is like being able to exercise a muscle which has been in a sling for a long time. So for me the examination is comparatively easy to pass. But for *you* the examination is so much harder and the degree conferred so much more obscure. . . .

113

I found it was a great help to work with another fellow preparing for examinations in college, even if he knew less about the subject than I, for there were always things he could help me with, in return for something I could help him with, and just the fact that we were working together gave comfort and strength. We will buckle to it for a long "grind," and if I should complete my course before you, which means that your exam will be even longer and harder, then don't give up; work all the harder. I think I realise how much harder it will be, but I count on you to do it. That will be your life's great opportunity, to live on when the weariness is so great everything in you cries out for "eternal leisure."

If that occasion arises, you must hear in it the supreme challenge and hold up your head and respond to it, and then when the time comes you will have lived a life infinitely more worth while than mine can be at best, because it will present so much larger an opportunity. It is because as a rule men's lives never have such an opportunity presented that they look to another life hereafter. But with a righteous struggle such as this, life would be complete. There would be no need for another, and if there is another, so much the better; but it can take care of itself and there is no need to bother one way or another about it.

Deepest love and affection always.

Royal Flying Corps,
Camp Borden, October 26, 1917.

Dear Mother,—

It has cleared a little in the last two days for short periods so I have got a little more accomplished, having now only about two hours' more work. This afternoon I went up to read ground strips. Calling up a station in the usual manner, I had him put out ground strips in the shape of a letter and then I would send down the meaning. This is a test to make sure you know them all, for they are the means of communication used from a battery to a machine in the air. I passed it all right. Some fellows take a card up with them with the meaning all written out, but that is not much use, for they will have to learn them some time and it is easiest now. I kept hoping, even as late as yesterday, that I might finish in time to get at least three days' leave; but it was no use, so I have given up struggling against the impossible and am taking things as they come now.

I have put in over fifty hours' solo flying now, so I am sure of my wings when I am commissioned. The wings are nice to have; but it is good I have been able to get so much time in, for every hour means that much better preparation. No two flights are just the same; the air conditions always vary, and of course each flight means a landing, which you can't have too much practice in.

I expect I can finish tomorrow or next day if the weather holds passable, and then I shall take a day in Toronto to get a few necessary things, and Tuesday we pack up to go, leaving early Wednesday. It will be quite a lot of fun, travelling in a big bunch together on special trains for four or five days. This is one more interesting trip I shall have added to the many during the last three years—practically every section of the U. S. and Canada and a trip to Europe. So many who have to go have never had such good fortune.

Deepest love.

Royal Flying Corps, Camp
Borden, Ontario, October 30, 1917.

Dear Father and Mother,—

... Oh, I am so glad to be leaving this place! I never hated surroundings more, not the cold or discomfort or the work, which I have really enjoyed keenly, but the unutterable loneliness of the scene, whichever way you look. The great American Desert was beautiful as I crossed it two years ago; but this flat, scrubby desolation has been awfully hard to ignore day after day. Any change will be most welcome.

I had become so used to having my feet pass from the stage of acute pain to numbness on every flight that I seldom minded it and would always stay up till a certain "stint" of time was ended or a test completed; for I was too anxious to finish to let anything interfere. Soon after coming down the feeling would gradually come back, but I notice finally that I must have frozen my feet and one hand on some trip, for they have been rather sore and deadened in feeling for about a week; not bad enough to be serious, but it shows it really is pretty cold up there when it is below freezing even on the ground.

Texas

R. F. C, Hicks Wing, School of A. G.
Fort Worth, Texas, November 4, 1917.
Dear Mother and Father,—

At last we are here. We got into Fort Worth last night, but weren't allowed off the train till after breakfast this morning. This camp is just the same size as Borden, but looks different in every way. So far as you can see in any direction it is absolutely a level plain. One could land anywhere in case of engine trouble. And the air is so calm and warm, not the least sign of a cloud or gusty wind, perfect for flying. Yet I am glad I had to learn under the difficulties of a small rough aerodrome and bad weather, for I am that much better off. . . .

The trip down was quite a trial because of the confinement. It is obvious that if they let three hundred or four hundred boys out at every station free to roam, we wouldn't have many left when we got here, so whenever the train stopped long enough we all got out and paraded for the exercise, but of course it wasn't much fun. And though most of the fellows were in the tourist car, I was lucky to be with a bunch in a Pullman, greatly overcrowded, however. Still we had lots of fun, and it was interesting country that we passed through—all new to me from St. Louis down.

The camp is about fourteen miles west of Fort Worth, as yet far from finished. They have n't any quarters or messing facilities for us yet, so we are camping in one of the hangars. But it is all such a great change and relief from Borden that I don't mind it in the least, and it can't delay us in our work, as they run that absolutely on a schedule.

Much love to all.

R. F. C. Hicks Wing, S. of A. G.
Fort Worth, Texas, November 6.

Dear Father and Mother,—

We are slowly getting a little more settled in our quarters, and the food is better now. They really had no provision at all for us the first day. We are living in a hangar, one hundred and fifty of us together, some music if you happen to wake up late at night! Water is the greatest difficulty,—it is hard to get enough to wash your teeth, let alone bathing; but I got a midnight pass to go into the city last night and had a good shower and swim at the Y. M. C. A. The lights, like water, are not yet installed, so we are using candles. But the wonderful warm clear days and cool fresh nights make up many times over for all limitations.

Last night we were the first R. F. C. Cadets in Fort Worth,, and we created quite a stir,—soldiers were saluting us, and people stared. I was talking with one soldier and he remarked in surprise, "I didn't know Canadians could speak English!" Another asked where we were from, and when I said, "Canada," he asked, "What State is that in?"

Our work is real work in this course. Very little flying, and that merely with our officer as pilot while we work the machine-guns. But this is the work that counts, for if you know your gun and can handle it your chances are practically sure of being on the right side. There are a great many lectures and much study, so I dare say I won't be able to write as often for a few weeks as heretofore; but I am on the last lap now with the shoulder-strap at the end—and then leave and home.

I'm hoping for some mail in a few days, as there is quite a blank during this change.

School of A. G.
Fort Worth, Texas, November 12.

Dear Mother,—

. . . . I am taking too much pride in my clear record thus far to let anything break it. I have never been checked up for being late on parade, dirty buttons, needing shine or shave, as almost every one has one time or another. That is one reason I was picked for a corporal. There are a hundred and fifty cadets in this course, and fifteen corporals, so that puts me among the first fifteen of the bunch. That doesn't mean much, and yet it is significant of what I have been aiming at in all my work, to be better than the average, that is,—as in my last year at college,—not only not be in the D or E class, and not in the C or good-enough average class, but in the B and A class, better than is absolutely necessary. For considering the curve of mortality, it is drawn to fit the average and indicates a certain percentage of that average that must be killed. Being in above-the-average class, the curve is no longer true, the percentage is far less. In the average class say you have a fifty-fifty draw, then it is as likely to be you as the next fellow. In this class you reduce the element of chance.

That, I believe, was one of Napoleon's plans. He made a plan considering all known contingencies, then in addition he gave it extra strength to reduce the element of chance, until its success could not be thrown in doubt even by something unforeseen. So you see it isn't any virtue in one to be trying for a good record; it is the desire to come back and enjoy my life, the family, the farm, etc., that gives the incentive. I knew I could learn to fly all right, but I wasn't sure of the gunnery, for that requires a different sort of skill; but I find I am beginning to get considerable accuracy and before I finish I shall get it good. Then let the Hun do his worst and I will go him a point better.

This gunnery is great fun, for we have so many different sorts of practice. The range work consists in plain target shooting, shooting at silhouettes of machines with aerial sights which allow for the speed of travel, etc.—that is, learning to give the proper deflection of aim so your bullets will cross his line of flight when he is crossing the bullets' line. Then we have surprise targets which pop up at certain intervals here and there, and you load, aim and shoot a burst. It is a training in quickness and precision. The idea of all this work is to make shooting as second nature as flying. We also have shooting at toy balloons and clay pigeons. Occasionally buzzards fly over and we all pot away at them. In the air we have the camera gun practice, flying the machine and shooting at the same time.

Then flying with a pilot while you stand in the rear cockpit with a gun on a swivel and shoot at a target towed by another machine, or silhouettes of machines on the ground, getting practice in diving down within a few hundred feet, firing a burst and soaring up again. You can see it is all very valuable and practical work and very interesting. Then in addition there is the work on the guns, the care and cleaning, and the knowledge of the action and name of parts, etc. All that I have absolutely cold, for that requires only study. We also have practice on jams so we can quickly fix the gun, spot the trouble instantly, and know just what to do. Air battles are a matter of seconds only; each second may mean a lifetime, so an absolute knowledge of the gun is essential. Some fellows borrow others' notes and skin through any old way, but that seems short-sighted to me.

In case you see reports of men being killed down here,—there have been three this week,—you don't need to worry about me, for in all cases it has been their own fault, "stunting" and taking chances too close to the ground, so they didn't have a chance to get out of their trouble before they hit. And in this gunnery course there is no chance of trouble, for it is straight work and no solo work, always with an experienced pilot.

Lots of love to all the family

U. S. Headquarters, Wing 1, Camp Taliaferro,
School of Aerial Gunnery,
Fort Worth, Texas, November 16.

Dear Mother,—

Plans are beginning to be more definite so I can give you some information. The course is to be about four weeks, ending Saturday, November 30th. Next day we leave for Toronto where we are commissioned, and I should be home by Thursday or Friday of the first week in December. I suppose the leave won't be more than ten days, so I will be leaving about the 15th. I am sorry we aren't to have Christmas together, but unfortunately Kaiser Bill won't stop for a vacation.

That means only two weeks' more work, and then for the commission. I certainly shall be glad to have it and to feel it was earned. I am getting along nicely in my work, getting considerable more accuracy: on several tests, being the best in my squad. It is going to take a good Hun to get me, if I know it.

November 19.

Dear Father,—

Yours of the 12th came, giving me the news of the family. I wish I could have been with you all on Beth's birthday, but if things turn out as I hope, I shall be home for Thanksgiving, and perhaps you and Os can get "leave" for the day so we can all be together for a memorable day. We had a preliminary oral examination today which I had no trouble with, and Friday night we shall be all finished. I shall be very proud of my commission, for it means much to be an officer in the first ranking branch of the British Army, to be one among the finest of men who have distinguished themselves so splendidly, being ready to have my chance, and having back of me three months of priceless, interesting and valuable training, development and experience.

Incidentally I will be receiving the sum, amounting with allowance and flying bonus to about seven dollars a day with a two-hundred-dollar equipment allowance to begin on, so I can settle up that Liberty Bond business with you and still be well fixed.

Had a nice long letter from Beth today with lots of home news. It is going to be terribly good to be home. I'm holding my breath in anticipation.

Much love.

Friday, November 23.

Dear Mother,—

Your letter of the 20th brought me great happiness today, together with the satisfaction of having completed successfully the last lap for a commission. We took our examination yesterday afternoon, and I feel that if I didn't receive the highest grade I was among the highest, for I absolutely know the subject.

In the evening the O. C. had each man come into his office, probably so he could associate the name and face together in writing out the report that goes over with us. He just asked a few general questions of no particular pertinence. Then he asked, "Do you think you know the gun?"

I said, "Perfectly, sir."

He said, "I should scarcely dare say that myself!"

"Then I should say," I replied, "that I know perfectly everything that has been given us in the course of instruction."

And I do, for I felt all along that effort expended now in learning the guns till, like flying, they require no thought to operate, would be like paying so much on my life insurance policy. To get extra sureness, when some of my friends realised I did know the work pretty well, they would ask me to explain a point, and going over and over the different points, explaining rather than being explained to, drove the whole business home, to stick. Then, when I had a chance I would ask my squad instructor to ask me questions to try and stick me. In this way I was able to find out what I didn't know and so get it.

In the actual shooting my record was near the top of my squad in every test, and in two it was at the top. However, we get a lot more opportunity to practice shooting in England, so I know with what I have had here as a basis, I can learn to do it well. Then, with a good machine, good flying, and good shooting, my chances are better than the average of coming back. In college, when I failed an exam you would say, "It is your old failing—rather be lazy and take a chance than make sure." If I do have bad luck you can have the satisfaction of knowing it wasn't because I left anything to chance. But when I look round the room, I can see the below-average fellows,—their chances are slim. Then I see the average, the fellows who did only what they had to do, somehow failing to see the importance of excelling. They have fifty-fifty chances, one as good as the other. Then there are the above-average fellows, a large percentage of whom should be able to tell their children all about it afterwards.

Some of course may have circumstances against them, but not because they neglected anything. These are the ones I want to be with. The O. C. planned to retain several as flying instructors, those with special qualifications of age, temperament, skill and good record, and I was gratified to hear that I was one of them. But I was glad to hear later that orders came from headquarters not to keep any from this course, so we can now go right over and get extra time in England before being sent over to France in the spring. If I was retained for three months, which is as long as is allowed, I would be sent to France almost immediately after arriving in England, for as spring approaches, more are needed. So this way I may have as much as two or three months' practice in England, before being sent to the front. More insurance.

I can't express to you how much I appreciated all you said in your letter. It is such an incomparable joy to feel I am coming up toward your standards; for it is only in this way that a son can repay his mother for what she has given him, literally everything. And it is going to make things so easy to feel that we are backing each other up through the fight, right side by side, regardless of the miles between us, for this bond diminishes any distance to nothing.

Beth wrote me that you were working over at Irvingcroft, so I understand why you had not written, for I know how hard you go at house-cleaning. You must not give more strength than the job is worthy of, for another job may come along deserving more energy and you won't have it to give. You must keep all you have, for when I come back after the war we will have so much to do, and I am afraid the war will be long yet, so be careful of yourself. It is needless to say how much I shall be looking forward to that day. . . .

My leave in any case is going to be as good as a *lifetime* to me, for I have been away long enough, and have come close enough to what is ahead to be able to prize it at what it is, a tiny foretaste of heavenly happiness we shall have when it is all over and we have earned peace.

Well, those the war doesn't kill with pain, peace will kill with joy, so what's the use of worrying which does it? Nothing like it. You have dipped me into the River of Styx of your boundless love so completely that not even my heel is left.

Before Sailing

En Route,
December 14, 1917.

Mother Dear,

I was sorry I didn't have things to say which would have helped you more when we said goodbye, but after all, words couldn't help much. You have got to think of the things it is going to mean to us all that I can be in it. If just the training has opened my eyes to so much, think what I shall get out of the real struggle with the daily association among fine men who are doing big things. We are going to get a great deal out of our letters, even if often they are delayed, and they will help to bring us close together in spite of the distance.

Even if I don't come back, it is all right, Mother, for you know we can't hope to gain such wonderful ends without paying big prices, and it is not right to shirk payment. I know you will come to the top and see all the many wonderful things to be glad for, and not grieve any more, and that you will accept bravely and gladly whatever may come, without worry or foreboding. And my chances are really good that I can return; for I have learned my work well and driven into myself a course of conservation, unwavering determination, which is going a long way toward bringing me back. I haven't relied on hunches or chance or luck; and if I had, I should have as good chances as any other. This way I believe better.

Oh, it has been such a perfect and complete vacation in every way,—not a regret, and unexpected happiness, so it is easy for me to go and do the very best that I can.

I doubt if you can read this, as the train is so rough. But I wanted to chat with you a few minutes and tell you I am so happy, so you can be glad. Bear up, Mother. Our fight is on, and we are going to win, you and I, no matter how hard it is. I'll try to drop a card at least before embarking.

Montreal, Canada
December 18, 1917.

Dear Mother,—

We did get in before noon all right and reported as directed. We were given transportation to St. John with orders to leave here tonight at seven. I understand it takes over a day to get there, so it will probably be Monday or Tuesday before we get on our way to sea. A week from this is Christmas Day, and allowing four days before I can cable, and a day for transmissions, don't expect to hear for about two weeks from today. And remember, if you don't hear, then there are countless reasons which we don't know about which might easily account for it, and you would hear if there had been trouble. So just be patient and don't worry. It is strain and worry that will wear on you and make you grow old.

Remember, they won't do any good, and I am looking forward to finding you fresh and strong on my return, so we can do the nice things together that we want to.

It is nice, in a way, and not so hard as I expected getting back again under orders, etc. For all these fellows I have gone through with are here and we are getting into the atmosphere again. And then of course I have the Happy Secret to carry with me which makes all so complete and satisfactory, and I know you are glad that it is so easy for me. I only wish there was something equal to it I could give you to help. But there is lots in it out of which you can get comfort and satisfaction, and I know you will look at these things and be brave and happy.

Montreal, Canada
Saturday Afternoon, December 18, 1917.

Dear Beth,—

Just a line before leaving here for St. John, where we sail. It is useless to try to tell you how much my vacation meant to me aside from the new happiness. For even though the kids were sick I liked being with them more than I ever did before. And I think the visit gave us an opportunity to get to know each other a little better. I appreciated the way you said goodbye to

124

me, it meant a lot—more than if it had been different.

I know what you are going through and have yet to bear and it gives me the deepest respect and pride in you. Sometimes it may seem as if you won't be able to go through with it all, but don't think of it *all*, for that is overpowering, just carry on from day to day. No one can get up enough strength to meet the whole thing, but some can scrape up enough for each day and I have confidence that you can. And now that the situation is here, I know neither you nor Mother, nor any of us, would have it different, for it means so much to us that we can be in it, in something bigger than ourselves.

I am so fortunate to have things turn out so unexpectedly happy for me and everything about the situation so perfect, as you pointed out, all the sweetness of this new joy with none of the pain of ruptured associations. I feel it is almost unfair for my going to be made so easy compared to other fellows, and the struggle you and Mother have to meet. Of course I want terribly to come back now, but if I don't, you and Mother can know, it was so easy to remain. I think I am going to do well, for this has put a new responsibility on me. I shall not be too cautious and hesitate in a vital moment. I feel well equipped and full of pep and so I'm not worrying or thinking about the outcome. I don't need to, for it will take care of itself.

You take good care of yourself and those nice kids, and if I am "detained" a while you tell them about their old uncle as they grow up and can understand, so they will know what we are trying to do for them and getting so much out of, ourselves. But I expect I can tell them myself.

St. John, N.B.
December 21, 1917.

Dear Father and Mother,—

We got in late last night, about ten hours late, and spent the night comfortably at this hotel, and we go on board this morning. I am told there are two first-class steamers going over, so I guess we shall have a fine trip and lots of fun. My cold is a thing of the past now, so I am feeling fine.

It certainly is cold up in this region. Yesterday morning as we travelled through the northern part of Maine it was 22° below. It made me feel as if I was going to the farm as we passed through long stretches of woods with deep, dry, clean snow piled high everywhere, and I enjoyed the trip greatly in spite of its extra length.

I wish I could be with you this day to cheer you up, but my thoughts are there even if I can't be. I know you will be in the swing and routine of things again and won't worry about me any more than when I was away in Texas. As I get back among the fellows again and look them over I can't help feeling as before, that my chances are really good and we shall all be together again when this is over. Perhaps even something will turn up so I won't have to wait till the end. Don't get impatient waiting to hear, for there are bound to be delays of one sort or another.

Have a really happy Christmas there all together, being glad that I am where I am, for you know none of us would want it different.

Loads of love to all.

Going Over

The Canadian Pacific Ocean Services Ltd.
R. M. S., December 22, 1917.

Dear Mother,—

I thought we should never get away! Running madly about after trunks and luggage, we got on board and didn't move from the dock till the middle of the *third* day. Although it is a small ship, it is good, clean, and they say seaworthy. My room is well forward, so there is no engine vibration, and I expect a 'very pleasant trip. Perhaps this note won't get to you. I am writing it on the chance it will be taken off at a stop we expect to make. Anyway it will do me no harm to try. Now you can easily see it will be some time later before you get letters back from the other side, because we are leaving so much later.

It is hard to realise it is a week since I left you all, for one loses track of time when doing nothing. I suppose before we know it we shall be over. I shall be glad to get settled at work again, for this doing nothing with everything ahead is rather trying. . . .

We have a wireless report that Kaiser Bill is making another peace offer. Wouldn't it be nice if we had this little cruise and came back again! No, now that I have gone this far, I want a chance to try out what I have acquired. Then, when I have got in some good licks, they can't have peace too soon to please me. It really may come, and some time it will have to come, and I believe I shall be around. Then for home, but now for the work. Remember, you aren't going to worry at delays and rumours,—wait for facts; they will be good ones that I am going to furnish you, so every day you will be more glad that things are as they are.

Much love to all.

The Canadian Pacific Ocean Services Ltd.
R. M. S. December 28, 1917.
Dear Mother and Father,—

If you received the letter I sent ashore at the first stop you will not have wondered why you haven't heard from me sooner. We are not allowed to send mail ashore that way usually, but the O.C. was going ashore, so he took it for me, though he may not have mailed it. It has been a long, tedious trip,—two weeks, I expect, from the time we first got on till we disembark. But in the worst weather, which was round Christmas, I was never seasick, and we have had pretty good fun, for in a crowd of men there are always funny things happening. We all read about the disaster at Halifax, but you had to see it to form any conception of how terrible it must have been. At the farther distances, just windows and chimneys were broken; nearer, roofs and walls were caved in; and then in the immediate area, a whole hillside was stripped as flat as if it had been raked, not even heaps of wreckage,—everything level. It must have been incredibly terrific.

The day before Christmas it began to get pretty rough, and that night the ship rolled so that it was impossible to sleep a wink, for it was a continual fight to keep from rolling out of the bunk. Half the ship was sick Christmas. They decorated the dining-room up a bit with paper and flags, but it only made the absence of Christmas greens the more noticeable. There wasn't one Christmas thing the whole day. They did give us turkey in the evening at dinner, and at our table we opened up a little champagne (Pol Roger 1904, only 14 shillings), which put some degree of life in us; but never again will I spend Christmas on the sea.

Overseas

The Royal Overseas Officers Club,
At the R. A. C, Pall Mall, London, S. W.
January 2, 1918.

Dear Mother and Father,—

Monday night I arrived in Glasgow. The day was not very clear, but the smooth rolling hills, green in spite of some snow and cold, were very beautiful as we came up the Clyde. You know it is the greatest shipbuilding port in the world and was very interesting to see. I came down to London with three others in a compartment, sitting up all night and no heat in the car. It was very uncomfortable and tedious, but I went to a hotel and last night got a good sleep. During the day we were busy at the airboard office getting our bearings. Yesterday being a holiday, I had to wait till today for my mail, and I was so very glad to find some there,—one from you each, one from Beth, and two from Grace. It seemed a very long while since I had seen you all, and these made the London fog seem lighter.

But I'm in no gloom, for we really are having a great time. We came down here, four of us, and became members by merely signing our names. One of the fellows had been told about it. It is a very large fine club, with Turkish baths, a wonderful swimming-pool, and all the conveniences of a most up-to-date hotel. It is so popular that they could not give us rooms, but instead, gave us an order on the Strand Palace Hotel, so we get a 15-bob room for 6 bob. We are given leave till Monday the 8th to get rested and buy clothing, etc. So this way we can have a good time, live in the best way and yet have minimum expense. The club, I believe, has been taken over by the military authorities for this purpose, and they make up the deficit.

The four fellows I am with are most congenial. One is H——
from East Orange, who spoke to us on the train platform when
I left. Another is a fellow from Baltimore; one of us is the man
who went through the S. of M. A. ahead of the others. He is
very amusing in the constant blunders he makes. After a final
one, tipping a barber 2 bob, I took all his money from him except some small change, and so I take care of him. The fourth
is an older fellow from Montreal. We are hoping we shall be
placed in the same squadron, but can't be sure, as the last draft
was very much divided up.

It was pretty soft this morning being wakened by a pretty
chamber-maid with a tray of tea and toast. This London life is
great stuff! Well, we may as well enjoy it while we can.

I suppose you began to wonder why you didn't hear from me,
but the trip was much longer than we expected. We get special rates on cables,—tuppence ha'penny a word,—so it doesn't
cost much, you see.

I'll write again toward the end of the week and tell you what
I am doing.

    Much love.

The Royal Overseas Officers Club
At the R. A. C, Pall Mall, London, S. W.
January 3, 1918.

Dear Beth,—

Your letter was most appreciated when I found it with several
others on my arrival.

I am relieved to know Mother has adjusted herself to my absence so well. It was hard for her to let me go, but when my
letters begin coming at regular intervals it will be easier for
her. And from all that I can gather I shall probably be here in
England several months, as they can do very little flying in this
weather.

There certainly is a difference in being an officer. Being a gentleman means more in England than in America. This club is
a wonderful place to be in; for it is very cheap to stay in, and
quiet and secluded,—far nicer than the best hotel in that way.
But crude as we may be in America in some ways, we certainly
know how to live comfortably, which they don't know here, or
in France.

Food is not unduly expensive, nothing to what it is in New York. There are certain things very scarce, however. They weigh out your insufficient allotment of sugar for tea far more carefully than we weigh gold. War bread in limited quantities is given, not really so bad as it might be. And not much butter in evidence. But nevertheless money has a sad way of melting. A pound seems to go as fast as a dollar, and until we begin securing our flying pay some of us are going to be pinched a bit. That will start in a few weeks though, so I shall get on all right.

I was interested in a number of Biblical references a fellow had coming over on the boat, which coincided in placing the end of fighting in the middle of February. He was so convinced that he was taking bets on it. I don't expect it then, of course, but if Russia keeps on quibbling, at least she can't be an active aid to Germany, and this next spring and summer may see something decisive of a military nature, at least make the end more in sight than it seems to be now.

H—— has a girl in Baltimore, and we make lots of plans how we are going to return—heroes, what? We have decided we shall be married in the R. F. C. dress uniform, which has blue trousers like the navy, except for a red stripe down the side, and a blue tunic cut on the lines of the regular army coat, with gold buttons, gold wings, sword, etc. H—— has decided that he prefers to fight the war here in London, and I agree with him that it would be ideal, but not for that "returning hero" stuff. One might think the war was just outside the city walls, however, judging by the thousands of officers one sees on the streets. But then, it is not strange, for they all come to London for their leaves.

Much love and remembrance to the kids.

> The Royal Overseas Officers Club,
> At the R. A. C, Pall Mall, London, S. W.
> January 6, 1918.

Dear Father and Mother,—

Really I have done disgracefully little these five days but sleep, but the rooms are so cold and the beds so comfortable and warm, it is most conducive to sleep. Friday, however, I had an interesting time. H—— called at the office of a business connection of his firm, and the junior partner asked us out to dinner and theatre Friday. We had dinner at the Oriental Club, which he said was a typical old British club. We met his brother there, a lieutenant-colonel attached to the protection of London from air raids, and he told us many interesting things. He was a man of about fifty, tall, stiff, very precise. He had spent the greater part of his life in India in civil and military life.

The club was interesting. Cold, barren, high ceilings, yet lots of atmosphere. The walls covered with great full-length portraits. After the last course of dinner they removed the tablecloth for cigars and port, and the table was a solid piece of mahogany. We went to the theatre and saw a musical play, exceptionally good music and acting. We may have it on the English in hotels, but they certainly have good theatres. Lots of room in the seats, a bar at the rear for between the acts. And the only place you see good-looking women in London is on the stage. There they surpass those on the French stage and on ours many times over. The tax is very high, yet every theatre keeps overflowing for long runs, filled practically entirely by officers back on leave.

Tomorrow we report again, and I shall feel much better when I can get at work, for this doing nothing gets on one's nerves. From what others say who have come over on previous drafts, we shall be in England about three months before you need begin worrying.

I am sending separately a copy about the R. F. C. which contains some very interesting pictures. You may enjoy it and pass it round the family. I have sent one to Grace also. I'm going to try for some more mail tomorrow. I hope I'll have some luck.

Much love to all.

Royal Club for Officers,
Pall Mall, London, S. W.
January 7, 1918.

Dear Ones,—

Today I reported at headquarters and was assigned to a camp about two hours outside of London in Hampshire near Andover. The squadron uses a type of machine which is one of the newest, large two-passenger, so your gunner protects your rear; fast, and yet slow landing ability. They have had the highest average for safety at the front, so I couldn't be better fixed if I had been asked my choice. I go down tomorrow and shall be glad to get at work again, as it has been so long since I have done anything. I shall be there two or three months, so you have no need to worry for some time; and when I do get to the front I couldn't be in safer circumstances.

England, January 10.

Dear Mrs. Cameron,—

Not having had a reply from "Sandy" for some time I thought I would write you, in case he has been transferred to some other station, and you can give him my address. For I hate to get out of touch with my old friends these days when there isn't much joy to anticipate, and happiness consists largely in reminiscing about the good old days at Cambridge and Westford, which already seem so long ago. I don't think Sandy knew quite how much I enjoyed those diverting and restful weekends which we occasionally spent with you all in Westford, a break in the Cambridge life, a little touch of family, and a taste of the country reminding me of the farm I love so much. I feel for the moment as if I were there, as I forget my surroundings in order to chat with you. I hope you will pardon me for doing so, and possibly you may be interested to know what I have been doing these several months.

About the first of August I joined the Royal Flying Corps and began training in Canada. There we flew the Curtiss machines, which are well qualified for the purposes of instruction. I remained there about three months, going about from one camp to another in the course of instruction, learning not only to fly, but quite a bit in connection with war, that is, artillery observation, reconnoissance, photography, bombing, etc. It was a wonderful experience, and the joy and exhilaration of flying is incomparably wonderful, quite unsurpassed by anything in the world, and, I can assure you, far safer and less trying on your nerves than, for example, driving into town from Westford on Monday morning in time for a nine-o'clock.

The first ride is confusing, and I felt a bit nervous, but since then, when the novelty of the sensation was removed, I have never had a nervous moment. Doing the stunts which used to seem so daring and spectacular is really simpler than shifting a gear in a car, and a loop or two before breakfast is the best tonic and appetiser in the world. Really I am not trying to appear *blasé* about it. It is all so easy and natural when once you have done it; there are no such things as acrobatics in the air, you never break a rule of gravity or nature, it requires no undue skill. Merely confidence in yourself and the machine, push the lever one inch or two, so, then so, and you have looped or stalled, or made a tail-slide, or a nose-spin.

And the wonder of the air when you are up above the clouds at an altitude of eight or nine thousand feet!—the clouds indescribably white and insubstantial on their upper side, the air free of the dust and moisture closer to the ground, which makes it seem thick and almost foul in comparison with this rare, clear space, which seems really to be vacuum. Sometimes these upper surfaces take on strange fantastic shapes—grotesque gnomes, you can imagine, grim fortresses, or dainty palaces of fairies, thrones of Olympus. One's imagination runs riot in these never-before-experienced surroundings.

Once as I flew along on the very surface of a slightly rolling cloud floor, my wheels lightly skipping, just touching from one small hummock to the next, it seemed as if it were some ancient Grecian deity in his dragon-drawn chariot. Then, shutting off the engine, a dive through the dense blindness, and out over the far-stretching flat country on which every field is laid out like an old-fashioned quilt. Long sweeping, graceful spirals and turns, a straightening out as the ground approaches, a gentle bump and short coast, and you are back again to the old solid earth, quite normal in spite of your mental vagaries a few moments before; they seem as unreal now as they did real before.

And so it is. You go up and fly in the very clouds at sunset, which are so gorgeously tinged at a distance on the ground, and find you can almost touch this intangible colour. You begin to feel of another world. Then you come down and feel ready to devour a regular "Cameron" dinner, very much of this world!

But I fear I have let myself get carried away, and it is difficult to convey any real understanding of the sensations to be had in flying.

The weather became bad in the fall, so we went to Texas for a month to finish the course, and I arrived home for my leave soon after the first of December. I spent two most happy and satisfactory weeks with the family and came over. It was a bit hard on Mother to have me go, but my sister writes me she has adjusted herself admirably to the situation, so of course I am very proud of her. For I learned in the summer I spent in France that it is you mothers who have the hardest fighting in this war; it was that, really more than anything else, patriotism, invaded neutralities, etc., altogether, which got a rise out of the easy-going old Briggs of Cambridge days. It is war on war that I am after, and it is my particular good fortune to be attached to a long-distance bombing squadron which has for its purpose the destruction of war-manufacturing plants. I shall be here for a couple of months flying different types of machines, and then we go across.

The trip over here was uneventful and long, but there were many friends I had made in the course of training who came at the same time, so it was quite pleasant,—all except Christmas. That day was awful, but it is over now.

I would give a good deal this minute if I could sit down at your piano for a little play, and then walk into the living-room and munch a chocolate and see you all; then get a good supper of eggs and shredded wheat and apple-sauce and things which I won't get quite so good till I am back there again some day— let's hope not too far off.

Those were such good times, and it is a great joy to look back on them. We must have a grand reunion when we all get back. Please give my very best to Mr. Cameron and the girls, and re-member me to the Abbots. If when you write Sandy next you will give him my address and ask him to give me the news of himself, I shall be very grateful.

Andover, January 10, 1918.

Dear Father and Mother,—

I came out here Tuesday afternoon and spent the first night at a little old inn. The town is not very large, but quite attractive, which always helps a lot, I think, to make one content. Next day I was billeted with another fellow in a private house, where we have a nice light room and are very comfortable. But if these English people would use half the coal in a furnace that they burn in a dozen separate fireplaces about the house, they would keep warm and there would be enough coal left to supply the flat for a year. It really isn't cold, but it surely does feel so, and that is what matters. But there is one time I always get warm.

That is in bed. I haven't been in an uncomfortable bed since I arrived in England. And the blankets are not only warm, but they are much larger than ours. Just the same, I am most grateful for the Angora when I first get in.

I have been attached to a long-distance bombing squadron, and I think it will be most interesting, for there is always some definite object to fly to and something to accomplish, while the scouts' work, though more glorious, is just flying about waiting for something to happen. If later I find I am not really going to like this I can probably arrange to change to the scouts, but I shall let the matter alone for the present.

I am getting very impatient for more mail. I have only had that which was here when I arrived. But it is quite likely that I shall receive some tomorrow.

We all eat at an officers' mess and get plenty of bread and sugar, etc., which is short elsewhere. But the only vegetables they seem to know about besides potatoes are cabbage and brussel sprouts. They have jam, but no fruit beyond an occasional apple. However, I am making out all right, though I dare say I shall be a bit fed up with three months here. Perhaps we shall have peace by then. I guess every one wants it pretty badly among the Germans as well as Allies. America doesn't know what it is to want it yet. For America it is like a nightmare in which you half know you will soon wake up, and may perhaps in time. But here it is no dream. If the Germans make a supreme effort this spring and it fails, then I think peace may be possible soon after. But unless every last effort is made by the Allies, the Huns might not fail, for I believe they all recognise this is their last chance. It will be interesting to watch.

Two summers ago Wilson was about as popular over here as Villa was in America. Now they use no limits in the length of their praise. His "war aims" speech made a great hit in Europe, greater than Lloyd George's. Just at present, America stands as high over here as she did low a year ago. . . . It is wonderful to be living in this age; there are big things going on.

But I hope our mail does come tomorrow. It is easy enough to make sacrifices for big things, but it is darned hard to go long periods without hearing about the little bits of things at home. I intend living quite considerably longer yet awhile, so when you write, tell me all the family gossip.

Dear Father and Mother,—

Yesteiday we had our flying kit issued to us, and it is most complete and good, worth easily a hundred and twenty-five dollars. There are flying-boots, very large, fleece-lined, rubber-soled, reaching clear up to the hip, so I shall have no more frozen feet, a large leather coat, fleece-lined, which will keep me warm in any wind, a fur-lined helmet that extends inside the coat clear down to the shoulders, fur mittens that reach the elbows, so that flying will be comfortable at any altitude.

I have begun flying one type of machine which is not much different from the one I learned on and shall have no trouble at all handling the other types we must fly. Yesterday two of the machines we are to fly at the front arrived and are being put together. They are wonderful big powerful machines holding the altitude record for the world, some 29,000 feet, and will climb up four miles in about half an hour. They certainly will be a joy to fly.

This bombing is particularly attractive to me, for instead of aiming to kill men, as in fighting on the ground or even in scout fighting, we aim to destroy war manufactories, material things made to kill men. Thus we are striking at the very base of war. And this is most satisfying to me. For I am not in here for the sake of international treaties or patriotism, but to make war on war, because two summers ago I learned how much worse it is than the mere killing of men. In this branch of aviation there is not the opportunity for personal distinction that there is in the scout fighting, but even if I do not return a hero I guess you won't mind much, and probably my chances of returning are better.

Meanwhile there is a great deal to be learned, all about the science of bombing, navigation and night flying, which will occupy two or three months, so all in all you have far less to worry about than we supposed when I left.

Oh, that was such a perfect two weeks, absolutely satisfying and complete in every possible way; and I live it over and over and it helps pass the time till some more mail comes. It seems as if some must come now in a day or so, for the other fellows have been receiving American mail the last few days, so mail is being forwarded, I expect.

You would have been amused yesterday, Father, at tea. One of the fellows—English, he was—came in and noticed we had toast instead of plain bread. "Oh, toast! I say, orderly, have you a few drippings, you know?" You can imagine the intonation. Instead of having butter we use a very good grade of margarine, but in asking for it at table we say, "Will you pass me the camouflage?" It has been much milder the last few days, so I have felt very comfortable, and things are easier now that I am back into the swing of work once more. If only some letters will come! But I expect you had a much longer wait, so I must be patient. Much love to all.

January 13, 1918.

Dear Father,—

I am not noticing the cold nearly so much now, because I am really in better health than I was on account of the colds, and also I guess I am becoming more used to it. And with the fine equipment that was issued us, flying is a real pleasure. It sure is different and good being an officer, for it makes things better in a hundred different ways. I am getting along well.

The few Canadians here with me have already in these few days made quite a reputation in the squadron, for we have nearly all had more flying hours than the English in the squadron at the same stage, and we learned on machines which are really quite a bit harder than those they learned on. So we are ever so much better off. They assumed, fellows with six or eight hours' solo, that as we had just come in we weren't much good, so they began telling us all about it. We didn't say anything, but the first day on the machine several of us went up and did a few loops, etc., and then came down and acted nonchalant. The O. C. of the squadron wanted to hug us all, for he said it was the first real flying he had seen in the squadron.

When you are thinking of me over there you may be sure my thoughts are right there beside you with love and longing, and I surely am hoping hard that next Christmas will see us *all* safely together, with this war over. That is optimistic, I fear, but I am going to hope for it just the same. Deepest love to all.

January 16 1918

Dear Mother—

From the way mail comes, I expect to receive mail about every two weeks, but when you don't expect it frequently, it isn't too hard to wait, and it is very exciting to have a whole batch come; you don't know which to open first, so you look for postmarks and get them all arranged, and then begin the feast.

Speaking of feasts, some one told me that at the Red Cross place you can buy empty boxes made for the purpose of filling and sending overseas to men in the army. They can tell you what the size and weight instructions are. If you could get me a small one that could go by mail, sent c/o of the Air Board, etc., labelled, as I am told these boxes are, "Soldiers' Comfort Box."

The work goes on as usual but slowly, partly because of weather, and partly because the English never will know how to do things quickly. The great marvel to me is how they have succeeded in doing as much as they have. First, they have no system at all; then, they have all system for the system's sake, forgetting the end, and it is just as bad. However, we move along slowly but smoothly in spite of it all.

I was sorry to hear Harold Bradley got rather badly mashed up the other day, nothing permanent or too serious, but uncomfortable,—an arm and a leg broken I believe; he was stunting too near the ground. He is at another squadron, about ten miles from ours, and I haven't seen him. But he was in a scout squadron where stunting is part of the requirements. We don't do it as part of the business in our squadron, so you don't need to worry about me; besides, I don't intend to waste myself. Cheer up, Mother, and don't worry. Even away over here, and freezing cold, I never knew so much happiness and content, for I have a good job each day, and a wonderful mother and a sweet girl to dream of each night.

January 25, 1918.

Dear Mother and Father,—

The day before yesterday they finished assembling two of the machines of the type we are to fly at the front, and one of the English fellows who has been here longest was given instruction on it all afternoon and then put back on one of the old machines till he could make better landings.

Yesterday morning I was taken up for ten minutes' instruction, made one landing, and allowed to go off solo. It is a wonderful big machine, a regular thoroughbred, as different from these other machines as a Pierce Arrow is from a Ford. And they are very careful of them, for they represent about, I should say, twenty thousand dollars, and with a little carelessness you could wipe out in a minute the work of skilled labourers for many months. So I appreciated their confidence in me, being the first pupil in the whole squadron to fly it alone. I think I gained their confidence by the way I brought in the machine I wrote about in the letter to Wilson yesterday.

Well, I took it off and went up for a while to try it out in the air and get used to it. Most machines have a very limited range of speed, having to land almost as fast as they fly. But this has a device by which you can regulate the angle of a certain plane, and so make the machine fly level, hands off, or climb, or glide down at an astonishing slow speed for landing compared to what it will fly at. You can land as slow as sixty and it will fly well over a hundred, and, with the engines which the machines are equipped with at the front, quite a bit faster. But, on account of the larger size and weight, a hundred and twenty miles in these do not seem much faster than sixty in the others, unless you pass one of them in the air, or fly down to the ground.

Then I made a few landings successfully, and went up about a mile and made several successive loops. The major was most delighted when I came in, for not even an instructor had stunted these machines here. But I have never seen such strength, such response to the controls, such a real engine. These are built for service, and you can have confidence in them, and it is a real joy to drive them.

After lunch I went up again and climbed to 16,000 feet,—that is over three miles. I noticed not the slightest difficulty in heart or breathing, and I believe that those who do have trouble, have it mainly from apprehension. At this height it was exceedingly cold, but keeping my head in the centre behind the cowling I was perfectly warm.

I flew west over the plains of Salisbury where so many famous battles of English history have taken place. Then down to Southampton and out away over the channel. If it had been a clear day I could easily have seen France from there. Then back I glided down a mile, going at times nearly a hundred and sixty miles an hour. Even in the air you could appreciate that was travelling some.

Then I levelled off, to rest my ears a bit. Then directly over the aerodrome I went into a nose-spin, that is, nose and tail vertical, revolving round the axis of the body like a corkscrew. I kept in that for a mile straight down, and found it delightful and not a bit confusing. In fact, I would glance at my altitudes to see how low I was getting, look at the air-speed indicator, see to the temperature of pressure gauges, look out on the revolving country, perfectly clear-headed and comfortable and calm in what, until it was understood, was supposed to be a fatal stunt. To come out I merely released all the controls and she came out and levelled off at once of her own accord. I have seen one or two loops over the aerodrome, but not a spin. Then the last mile I glided down in long graceful spirals and turns and came in.

Then I found the camp, all work stopped, standing round watching. The colonel of the wing himself was there, and complimented me on my flying—"Splendid exhibition, Adams." He is the funny former-actor-colonel with the monocle. He even removed it to have a look at me, for he can't see with it on! Two or three of the Canadians were asking me how she flew, and they said they were glad I had shown up some of these "lead-swinging" Englishmen. Lead-swingers are those that stall along, doing as little as they possibly can, hoping the war will be over before they finish. There are quite a lot of them. You see, the best of them are already over there or dead.

Flying this machine graduates me, so my papers are to be sent in at once, and now I shall draw full pay, plus flying pay, and have full pay not drawn since I was commissioned, made up from that date. If it goes through by the first of the month I shall be comfortably fixed and be able to get a few things I need very badly.

I have only one more hour to fly on this machine now, a few simple ground tests in machine-guns, etc., and I shall be finished. It ought not to take more than two or three days more. Then I go to the Aerial Gunnery Squadron in Scotland near Glasgow, I believe, for a week or two, and then I'm ready for business in France; where, I trust, I shall be able to do some creditable work, for I do feel very well prepared. With such a machine you need have little worry. I mean that.

I received a card from Cousin Fred in California, and a few such very fine letters from Grace, so all in all I am very happy and eager to go over and deserve some of the good fortune that has been given me.

England, January 26, 1918.

Dear Beth,—

I am very pleased with the way I have been able to get along, for I expected to drag out here till the end of March. At present I am the farthest advanced of anyone in the squadron; in fact, the first clear day, I can finish in an hour. So, accounting for delays of one sort or another, I ought surely to be at the front by the first of March. I certainly hope so, for it is going to make things easier all round.

I believe you will find it the same with Oswald; once he is on the line, the long wearing dread of that moment will have passed, and while your anxiety will be great, it won't wear on you the way this delayed evil does. And he will be easier in his own mind too, and cease to care about casualty percentages. The closer you get, the easier it becomes, for the less you think of it.

I have never been happier than now with the satisfaction of Her letters and the consciousness of the treasure that is mine, the deepest bond that these experiences have meant with you all and home, and the keen anticipation of the great adventure in the near future, with its great opportunities.

Much love to you and the little ones.

P. S. Tell Os I shall be driving a 400 Rolls Royce. Some class!— what?

January 27, 1918.

Dear Mother,—

... I have now only to wait for a clear day to finish just an hour's work and I will be done here. I am so pleased, for I am ahead of every one else in the squadron regardless of how long they have been here, and have won the confidence of the instructors as well as several fellows who have asked to go up with me.

When one pupil is willing to go up with another it is quite a mark of confidence, for generally you feel nervous unless you are with an instructor or driving the machine yourself. And when I get to France I am determined it shall be the same way. Before I finish I want to be the first man in the squadron. It is best that way. You know it is the last man the Huns always watch out for.

But you mustn't expect immediate advancement as in the case of Oswald, for our work is done more in squadrons than as individuals; it is team work, so I won't be winning distinction. However, if I can hold up my position in the team and play with them I shall be content. . . .

January 30, 1918.

Dear Beth,—

Your letter of the 7th came today and I can't tell you how much I appreciate your writing me, for letters mean at least double what they ordinarily do, in this situation.

I am feeling rather badly off tonight in consequence of a most unfortunate accident today in which I was really a contributing cause, if indirectly. You see, I was the first pupil in the squadron to fly one of the new machines, and I gave a pretty good exhibition to these Englishmen of what American blood can do. So another Canadian next furthest advanced to me naturally wanted to try the same things, and as a result, the machine collapsed, both wings falling off 4000 feet up, and he was killed. A perfectly wonderful fellow,—jolly, and liked by everyone.

You wouldn't have felt so badly about it if he had been shot down at the front, for there is so much satisfaction in such a death, or even if he had been killed doing something foolish or stunting close to the ground. Those accidents happen frequently, and we just shrug our shoulders and carry on. But this was absolutely no fault of his. Furthermore, it happened in the same machine I had stunted in, and, while these are war machines, built to stand anything, I feel perhaps I may have strained something which gave way under the stress this time. Of course I am in no way responsible, but it does bring it pretty close to me, and I feel terribly about it.

Fortunately I finished all my work in this squadron today so I won't have to go up for some time, and I guess I shall feel better later on. It is very gratifying that I was the first to finish, for there are a lot of English fellows that have been here several months, and it has taken me just three weeks including much delay by bad weather. But it is really all a matter of pushing yourself,—that is, being on the spot when there is a vacant machine or any work to be done.

It was quite amusing yesterday. You see, the colonel of the wing was on the aerodrome the other day when I was up in the new machine for the first time, and saw me stunting, which quite delighted him. So he learned who I was by name. Then he said, "When you finish, come to me and I will give you four days' graduation leave."

"Pardon, sir, but if I can get right on to the gunnery squadron I had rather waive the leave, as I am anxious to get out to the front," said I.

At first he was inclined to think it a pose,—he couldn't grasp the point of view; but he was quite delighted when he realized I meant it.

However, the next course may not begin for a week or more, so I may take a leave and rest here a few days. I haven't enough spare cash to go up to London for more than a day or two, and I do need a little rest. . . .

I have now only this two weeks' gunnery course and I shall be a complete Service Pilot, and hope very much that, with the delays of training and all, I may be in active service by the first of March. I may have to wait a while for a vacancy, but at least my training will at last have been completed, so I'll have that satisfaction.

February 1, 1918.

Dear Father,—

. . . Having finished up the work here, I am enjoying greatly a few days' rest from the absolute regularity of the past three weeks, Sundays included. For you do get tired of getting up every single morning in the dark and cold, not even having one day a week on which you can lie in bed a bit longer. I don't know how long it will be, but I hope soon, when I can go on and do the two remaining weeks' training; after which I shall be a full-fledged service pilot, and the day I set foot on France will be surpassed only by the day I once more walk into 32 Llewellyn Road. I am sure you and Mother feel the same about it.

I had an interesting experience today, going to the military funeral of one of the Canadian fellows who was killed the other day through collapse of his machine. He was a splendid type of fellow, and it was a shame that he should go, through no fault of his own, when he was so nearly finished. We formed up; practically every officer in the station was there, a fine tribute to the fellow. He was placed on a gun carriage drawn by four horses, preceded by a band playing a slow march, and flanked by two files of armed soldiers. The service was held in a church and completed in the cemetery adjoining. There the soldiers fired their volleys and the buglers blew a call, and as we walked away, each of us stepped to the grave and saluted our comrade.

No man could ask for a finer service. It was impressive, solemn, dignified and genuine. . . . To be working at a worth-while job of any sort is satisfactory, and this in particular. And to make it all easy I have the continual consciousness of the thoughts and interest and love of you all. And also there are the many little material reminders,—the cigarette holder from Howie, the letters that I read over, the pictures which I have of each of you. And every evening after tea when I come in for a quiet evening before the fire, remove my wet shoes and put on the "comfy" slippers and wrapper Mother provided me with, I couldn't be better off. I certainly am awfully lucky.

Love to all the family.

Thursday, February 7.

Dear Mother and Father,—

It has been nearly a week since I wrote, but, as I have been doing no work, there was little to tell about, so I have spent more of my time reading. I am getting fed up with this doing nothing, but I can't get on to the next squadron till the latter part of next week. However, it has been good for me, for I have not had to stand round for each day in the cold and wet, and it has abolished the last trace of cold which hung on mildly ever since I left home. And it has been fun to feel free of the regularity,— quite like the old Cambridge days when I could read or write as late as I wished, knowing I could sleep in the morning. . . .

This week I have really seemed so far off from the war that at times it was difficult for me to realise I was in any way connected with it, for I have drifted into the state where mental interests were the main pleasure,—reading, writing, philosophizing. I am glad I had the opportunity, however, for it gave me a chance to think out one or two questions which I have held off for several months, being engrossed in the more active work. . . . But now these matters are shaping themselves more clearly and definitely, and I can put all my energies in the real work without distraction. . . .

This regular fare is good for one even if it does become monotonous—potatoes, meat and brussels sprouts (without vinegar) or turnips alternating for lunch and dinner, followed by a sweet, as a bit of cornstarch pudding with a quarter of a preserved plum by way of flavour, or some tapioca. It keeps one well and you can get your fill, but in that dim uncertain day when I set foot in the home, with all restrictions done with, I know what I shall choose to eat. It is funny how one's world becomes fenced about in this sort of life. You think of your work, talk of it all day long, discuss rumours about it, dream of it. Then you stop and say, Let's go eat. You work your stomach, and not much concern about your soul. But that is a good healthy way to live.

A year ago I was home with you all during the midyear period; now everything is so completely different from that life,—the change in situation, circumstances and attitude. I often feel as if I was sound asleep in a dream,—not a bit bad either, for it is either one of those dreams you can't remember when you wake up or when you do remember it will be a dream With such a happy ending. It makes it very easy. Nothing, such as discomforts physical or of the heart, seems to penetrate inside the blanket of sleep, and what you can't have in real dream is here, the foreknowledge of a happy awakening.

Sunday, February 10, 1918.

Dear Father and Mother,—

It is a perfectly wonderful springlike day, warm and clear, and some violets on the lawn below my window are in bloom. This certainly is a strange climate.

I am going up to town tomorrow to get a few things I need, and next day go on up to the next squadron for a two weeks' course, after which I shall be entirely finished ready for service. Then I return here probably to instruct, and wait till there is a vacancy, when I shall be sent out. That can't come too quickly to please me, but there is no telling how soon it will be; it might be only a few days, or it might be a month or more. . . .

I expect to find quite a bit of mail uptown (London) tomorrow, as I wrote Cox to hold it about a week ago, and so am anxious to get there. No one here can understand why, for a week and a half perfectly free, I have not spent the time in London. But I have read a number of good books, had a fine rest, and have had to spend no money, and what I save now going without what they call a good time will be repaid many times over when I spend it according to my plans.

Much love to all the family.

In Scotland

Turnbury, Ayrshire, Scotland,
February 19 1918

Dear Father and Mother

I haven't written since leaving London because I have been working pretty hard and felt ready for bed early. This is the best place I have been in yet, a wonderful big hotel surrounded by a famous golf course right on the edge of the sea, from which Ireland can be dimly seen. It must have been a very gay place in the days before the war. Cousin Jack visited it as one of the points of a golfing tour he took several years ago.

For the first time since coming in contact with this army I am in a place in which the management leaves nothing to be desired. No time wasted, good instruction, much work accomplished. I feel I have gained quite a bit of accuracy and second nature in the handling of the guns,—ever so much more than what I got in longer time in Texas. But, much to my sorrow, just as I felt I was about completed, I received orders to proceed to another squadron back near where I came from when I finished here. It is for a further course in bombing, which will be valuable toward doing more accurate work in the field. But I am disappointed, for I hoped to go out by the first of March.

Judging by indications, it is going to be interesting out there this spring and summer. Lots of action and movement, so we won't get bored staying in one place doing nothing. You see, home and peace are such good things that a hundred little reminders of their absence in a day make me want home very much. This generates a lot of energy which will flow out naturally when I am at work toward those ends. But meanwhile I seem to move so slowly. . . .

Make Line keep at the pace. To think of the pace this war has required with never the slightest slackening, when thought of as three and a half years, means little, but when thought of as so many years of twenty-four-hour, sixty-minute days of supreme deadlocked effort, never a relaxation or breathing spell and all on such a titanic scale, that is what surpasses comprehension. When anyone slackened a bit it meant disaster, as in the case of Russia and Italy. It has meant that all of the millions composed of separate individuals in the field and at home have stuck hard at their jobs, putting in always a little more effort than the day before.

Reports in our papers from America are a little more optimistic in tone, but nevertheless, even though tremendous things are being done, they are awfully slow, and every minute counts. But they seem to be gathering a momentum which once started nothing can stop, and that is what we want.

We don't want to stop till the job is satisfactorily completed, but it is a big job; some of its proportions will be sure to be larger than any one conceived of, I believe, in the next few months. It is going to be great to be in on it, so tremendous that the thought fairly sweeps one off one's feet. It puts all of life on such a simple balance; here is a tremendous bit of work to be done which completely obliterates the little things of life which always seemed so important in the past. All one has to do is to give all his energy, just put everything in with one simple sweep, and when every one has done the same, the job will be finished, and the gain is so much bigger than what it may cost in these little things that they don't have to be even thought of.

I have often wondered what we shall do when it is over and we go back to the little things. I don't think the new growth and breadth it gives will be lost in a reaction of apathy. I believe after the war this energy will keep on and will never be lost. It will be turned toward making the little things of life bigger in each individual's case, and we shall see a rate of progress and achievement in the peaceful work of the world never before approached.

I enjoyed Mr. Pringle's letter with its farm concerns. It makes one feel attached to something substantial to know the old things are going on—getting out firewood, and pulp, and so on. So old Colonel is gone. He certainly was a good old animal and gave us lots of service. I remember how we used to alternate week by week with him and Madge and Belle in the old days when we drove to school ten years ago. It doesn't seem so long as that, for that winter is so vivid to me,—Miss Davy, Carol, Line and I together. I can even remember the toothache Carol spoke of in one of her letters to you. The work in the woods, Sid Clarke with his winter growth of beard, the daily lunches with Auntie, Uncle Dan and Grandpa Kilburn,—they all are so vivid to me. I can hear their voices and see little gestures. Uncle Dan and his inevitable newspaper, Auntie with her bills at lunch, Old Colonel reaching out a bit on the last stretch coming home from school in the early twilight of the winter months, the light of the library lamp shining out, with its promise of home, warmth, supper, family, content.

When these things abide, as with me now, they aren't dead, they are immortal, living, real, and in them is such sweet satisfaction. That is why I have been so determined about living with you at Irvingcroft when I come back, so when things begin to drop out of your lives, we shall have the home running to give a basis to keep all these memories alive, and new interests ever growing to keep life ever full—our nurseries, grandchildren, reunions, etc. And if for any reason I can't be the one to help bring this about, there is all the rest of the family, and you must all keep as close together as possible and carry on the Adams family just the same, for if I am anywhere that is where I shall be, at Irvingcroft and the farm always. But I shall see to it that I am actually there, never fear.

It is great fun from time to time as I write in my "line-a-day" book to see what I was doing a year ago. I notice just a year ago Father made a flying trip to Littleton to settle some of Uncle Dan's affairs, and I had dinner with him on his way up at the Parker House, and again two days later, breakfast. I used to enjoy those briefs visits so much, as it was a chance to have a chat with him, and incidentally get a good meal as a break from the Cambridge fare. My, what a break such a meal would be now! But it will keep, and be all the better for the wait when I do get it. . . .

Well, this letter has gone on to considerable length, and I guess I have spoken of everything I had in mind. I am in the best of health and feeling fine. The life is very healthful, even if it gets monotonous in the food, etc. And I am very, very happy and content; the little actual unpleasantnesses and separation feelings I don't let get inside at all, and the thoughts about you all and home are so vivid and happy, and your letters and love are such a comfort. And it's a good job. I'm only a bit impatient to be at it. So you have no need to worry about my welfare or happiness.

Deepest love to all.

February 21, 1918.

Dear Father,—

Today I finished all the instructional work here, and have only a couple of tests to pass off in the air before I go. Each day a group of fellows comes in and another goes out after a maximum period of two weeks, so there are a lot of groups in process of passing. They allow them four days to pass off the air tests, to provide for bad weather, for you can easily finish in a single day if it is clear. But if it isn't clear at all, you leave when your time is up just the same, and it doesn't much matter, for they are not important.

In the old days of college, when a man received a high mark and mine was just passing or average I accepted it as a matter of course, thinking that the high man received his mark because of superior inherited brain power, and I was meant to be only average. There seemed such a distance between us that it never occurred to me to attempt to catch up to him, it was preordained otherwise.

And yet, ever since the double shake-up I received in the early part of last July I began to make the effort to move out of the deadly limitations of the middle lot and was astounded to discover, in the various phases of my training in Canada and Texas, that the high man had probably little better brain than mine. It was merely a matter of seeing that the bonds holding me in the middle class were bonds of imagination and it only required moving one's feet to step out of the protecting but crushing crowd. So I began to go up nearer the top in various examinations and in the flying and found it is not a matter of superior mentality or any such thing, but merely more desire, more will. I figured that war is a risky business, but the risk was largely chance. Consequently, if I could master my particular

151

job in all its branches I could reduce the element of chance to a minimum. You see, I have great incentive to return, so it doesn't take much will. But all in all I think it has been a real discovery for myself, and that I can profit by the same procedure in my work when I come back.

It seems to me now that there is nothing impossible or out of reach if *imagined* obstacles coming from one's own mind are got rid of, and if one can stretch his imagination beyond what he supposed were the limits of his capacity, and see "big." Then it is a simple matter of getting up and going after it with a will. I think my experiences have taught me to see things in a larger way than I ever could before,—the bigness of the forces in this war. And searching for the good in it, and some of its fundamental causes in human nature, and its outcome in generations to come, has all stretched my mind a bit to grasp it.

Then also, more concretely, the new spaces I have run from high altitudes, the new breadth which comes in moving in three dimensions, the sense of terrific force when moving through the air at such new speeds. "Like sixty" was the idiomatic expression of speed, a limit of our previous experience. Yet I have moved at sixty and a hundred more on top of that, when, protected from the force of the air, you could feel it in the bursting feeling it gives your head, and the fearful roar. Then the new sense of utter abandon and freedom in falling. We used to jump into the hay from ten to fifteen feet safely. I have let the machine fall its natural way when uncontrolled, a nose spin, for a full mile down vertical. These new things are beyond all previous experience, beyond the limiting wall beyond which we don't see because we don't know we can look till victory. These have all broken down limits in one place or another, so that when I come back and start other work, it ought to be easier to step over the apparent limits.

This isn't much of a letter as letters go, but what I started out to say is, I received the highest mark in the examinations of our group of eighteen today, so you can see there is sound basis when I assure you that you need not worry about my welfare. This is substantial evidence of change. If I am better than the average here, I should be better than the average Hun as well. So you must not worry and must only feel joy that I am having the great privilege of being in the biggest thing in the history of the world.

Turnbury, February 22.

Dear Beth,—

Another of your good letters came today—the 30th of January—and you have a remarkable ability to put a deal of news and satisfaction into one envelope, quite after Ben Franklin's style of conversation, to consider what interests the other. And I appreciate your writing at all, for I know how busy you are and how much else you have to think of.

It is tantalising that Oswald was required to move away before it was time to go for good. It is hard, but it can't be helped, and it does mean more interesting work for him, I believe. But all this training uses up so much time, and time is so valuable out there, it makes one very impatient to move so slowly. And, valuable and necessary though it is, training seems so insignificant a work in comparison with the real thing. I'm afraid I have another month yet, and I had hoped so much to get out by the first of March. But after all it doesn't much matter—a month or two, for it looks as if things will start out there pretty soon now, and once they begin there will be no let-up till something breaks. Things will be hot, I expect, and terribly interesting, for they will be on a larger scale and more continuous in action than ever before. If Germany attacks, which the Allies hope she will, she can't stop, and the strain will break her back. The question whether she will or not will be answered soon.

I interested myself the other day by trying to analyse the spirit which has actuated each country to fight in this war, the spirit which is the consummation of nationally characteristic human nature. The German seemed to be the spirit of a big, husky, mentally limited son of the big man in a small country town, a fellow who has a strength and position earned by his father, but which he is too limited and too arrogant to know how to use worthily. The American Spirit as I see it from speeches and editorials, etc., is the spirit for a simple principle, believed in coolly and consistently, the principle of a business man who deals honourably because all must if there is to be any security and confidence in the market.

The Colonials have the spirit of a perfectly independent son, who supports his mother out of free loyalty to his filial bond. The English spirit is a pride in their traditions which were made by Drake and Wellington and Gordon, etc. It is not an

153

unworthy pride. With France it ceases to be a spirit and becomes a *soul*—the soul you can see so near the surface in a person who has suffered almost beyond human endurance and has risen above and become strengthened by this suffering. It will never die.

Isn't Russia ridiculous? "No, I won't make peace on your terms because they aren't fair, but I don't want to fight any more. No fair hitting me now; I have my fingers crossed."

I haven't heard a bit of real music since I left New York, except light stuff. All the Revues are a composite of Broadway two years old, and the musical shows are generally superior to American. That is, the English can't write classical stuff or popular stuff, but are pretty good in the middle-class music. "*Chu Chin Chow*" is a show based on the Arabian story of *Ali Baba and the Forty Thieves*, and there are some catchy things in it. There is a march which would make a wonderful national marching song—a great swing to it and much connotation of a great moving body. If I can get a copy of it sometime I will send it over.

I remembered it was "Howie's" birthday on the 14th and wanted to send him a cable, but honestly didn't have the kale. He will be about as big as "Day" was, when I get back, I expect.

I haven't been at Lilburne, that is another camp. I was at Andover, and go next to Stonehenge down in Hampshire.

Well, the time is getting on, so I must stop.

Much love to the kiddies and all.

With Palms Out

Turnbury, February 23.

Mother Dear,—

Your letter of the 4th came today, mentioning one you wrote in Boston which is being held at Cox's, and I shall get it when I go to London in a day or two. I am very anxious to read it and hear all about your trip to Boston in detail, for of course I am very interested about it.

I am afraid, Mother, you are taking things much harder than you need, the tantalising slowness of things at home, the bad administration, etc. It does no good to get worked up about them, for it makes one feel so impotent, and yet it makes the desire to effect some change so keen that one can't be happy, and being unhappy won't help. Many things are discouraging, and yet if you don't look at them too closely but stand off and see them as a whole, then you can see how really much has been done, and that it is all so new and on such a scale that it can't be done all of a sudden; the men in control are not used to such dimensions and so temporarily cannot think in such large numbers, but it will make them grow as the work does. On such a tremendous scale, where so many complexities are involved, it would be impossible for the whole thing to be managed properly, efficiently and swiftly all at once. But it will come about in time; it is all the time gathering up momentum which once started cannot be stopped.

The Allies are still very strong and can well keep going till America is completely ready. If America were nowhere in sight, the Allies might be discouraged, for, though they could not be beaten, it would be a long costly struggle. But with the sure knowledge of the ultimate unlimited power which America

155

will furnish, the whole morale is braced; they say, "Not only will we win, but we will win decisively." They pluck up their courage and can do even more than they normally would, and it doesn't matter if America doesn't start for six months or a year; once she does, it will be with a strength that can't be resisted.

Over here, after going on four years, things are often mismanaged, and valuable time wasted, yet all in all there is always slow but certain improvement. So it will be the same there. Don't let an immediate difficulty shut out, by its narrowness, the whole truth which can be seen by standing off at a distance. Coal is short, but that is not so much present-day mismanagement as conditions brought about by bad management and financial exploitation long before the war. It is a nuisance and a discomfort, but it will be straightened out in time. You know what meat-eaters and tea-drinkers the English have always been. Then to have but a few ounces of meat per week and often drink their tea with little or no sugar, is bringing the sense of war pretty close, yet it really is remarkable how little complaint and criticism there is.

You know how natural it is psychologically for people to think everything is wrong when something close to them, a lifelong physical taste, is meddled with, even if there is no direct connection. I think the way rationing has been accepted in England is one of the most encouraging things I have found. There is enough food but none to waste, and it is very regular, so one often wishes for just one feast of everything that can't be had. The fact that the situation is accepted so well speaks well for the way things are going. Of course they are more used to the idea of privations of one sort or another here, but America will get used to it in time. So when trying conditions come, and evils are revealed, you must hold them in their right value and not let them depress you. And never let things get into you personally. It is one thing to think about them, and another to get all heated up about them.

I go about as it were, *hands with palms out*, all about my heart, holding things outside of it. I am conscious of things I don't like, or discomforts sometimes, and things I wish could be true, etc., but I won't let them get into the inside where they hurt. If I can change them, I can do it just as well keeping them outside, and if I can't change them, well, what does it matter, it's outside. It doesn't make me indifferent to things which deserve consideration, merely insensible. You must do this, it's not hard, and you will find how much more quickly a day goes by, and after all how pleasant it is. So much for your concern about outside things.

Of course, being my mother, you feel concerned about me; but, except for just missing me, I don't want you to have another uncomfortable feeling in your heart, no worry about my health or comfort, or happiness, nothing of this sort. For any limitations of physical comfort are so ridiculously slight, especially compared with most, that it would really be good for me if I had more. And little petty annoyances are good for one's self-control; besides, as I said, I don't let them get inside. I have never been in better health. And I am completely content, for it seems as if I was never so rich or ever hoped to be. I have absolutely nothing in the world to ask for, for myself. My friends and family have never meant as much to me, and you are all so good to me. And in addition, the interest and satisfaction of my work is of such a nature that nothing that can happen matters to me.

You see you have no need to feel anything but gladness for me, so no more must you have any troublesome feelings in your heart except harmless missings which doesn't hurt when you know I am happy as I am. Don't say to yourself, "I mustn't let him see my depression or worries." Don't even get all braced and say you *won't* let yourself feel them. Just relax and *don't* feel them. Even when I'm Out There you mustn't feel any dread or worry. We get better food out there and are done with the petty things of training, and we will be right at the real work, so I shall be even happier than now. And if it should happen that—I just stopped being conscious, it wouldn't matter, because there was no regret and no dread, just perfect content.

And you will not dread any such event, for it is not a bit likely to happen. My examination mark hasn't been reached yet by the two groups which have passed out since my group. It was 94%, the average on all the tests we had, and they never give much higher. But if the *event* came you may miss me, but it won't hurt, for there will be no vain regret, because I am so perfectly content. So remember, Mother mine, you are going to relax, begin at once and keep it up, and people will wonder at you, that you are so serene and can do so much because your strength isn't being wasted by groundless or ineffective troubles, and when they ask your secret you can say that we are both so content with our situation as it is, that one can't be otherwise than serene.

You spoke of being more conscious of the grim realities than heretofore. To me the grim things somehow fade into unrealities in comparison with the realities of the heart and mind which are so vivid to me. I spend so many long happy hours with you all every day that my heart is completely filled with them, and I am very happy. I am glad you sent the little farm album, for so many of my hours are spent over it. I often go way back to the days when we were kids, with Ned, and the Blodgetts and Miss Noyes, over at Hilltop, and again later at the knoll when Vincent and the Platts and the slews of kids gave plays and had picnics. There *isn't one single unhappy memory* anywhere in the whole review. And I often roam there in the future planning the things I shall do and the fun it will be to show all the corners to Grace, the little trips we can take to Lost River, etc. And those drives up back of Harvey hill, and down into Lyman, etc. That wonderful ride we had with Betty and Mrs. Dodge was such fun.

It doesn't do any harm to live in these things at this time if I wish, so long as I do my work well, does it? You see, I never realised what a happy life you had made for me till I had this chance to get away and look at it. Now when I come back I shall be able, I hope, to give some of it back to you, because I think I know better how to do it. I sometimes feel as if I am taking too much good out of such a rotten thing as war. But still if we all do, then it will be worth the cost, and there must not be another, because it isn't fair to mothers. You must tell me all the feelings you have. Don't hide them, but do abolish them. . . .

London Again

The Royal Club for Officers,
Beyond the Seas.
At the Royal Automobile Club
Pall Mall, London, S. W.
February 26.

Dear Father,—

I came back to town last night, arriving this morning rather fagged after sitting up all night. Of course I slept some, but you know what it amounts to. Still, there is a war on, so what does it matter? We reported at the Air Board and were given instructions to proceed tomorrow to cross over, and over there we will be told where to go.

I was a little bit afraid we might be sent to Italy, where it would be novel and interesting of course, but not on the titanic scale of things as in France. I had to do considerable hustling round to get all my errands done, but I succeeded all right. I am having a nice uniform made to change into from this same old one which I shall keep for work only, as it is getting pretty badly spotted Up with engine oil. The pilots out there take pride in the signs of use their work uniforms show, the blacker the better. The new one I'm having made is of the "Universal" type, the turn-down collar, big pockets, etc., which officers in the other branches wear. It is perfectly regulation, and nice to have the change and additional comfort. I also bought a good substantial pair of heavy top boots for service there. And several other smaller items completed my immediate needs for which I was obliged to call on you. But my name has just gone through the *Gazette*, so by April first I can send a draft back to you and we will be squared up.

I found several letters for me at Cox's and it made my advent to town extra pleasant. One from Wilson, Mother's from Boston, and a couple from Grace written at that time. I can't tell you what a comfort and joy the frequent letters from you all mean to me. I have never known anything like it, and it makes me very happy all the time. I'm so glad you had a good chance to see Grace while in Boston, for it is easier to get to know people if a little time elapses and you can see them again for a second time. . . .

This afternoon I ran down to Andover to get my trunk which I had left there. I had less than an hour between trains, but it gave me a chance to see several of my friends that I crossed over with in December. They are all still there and due for another month or six weeks before they even go to Turnbury, because, as is always the case, new requirements are always being created. It made me very glad that I had escaped when I did. For it is in the nature of an escape. While these practices and tests are valuable, they are not essential, and take months to go through, and at the end they are not as effective as after a week at the front.

I am spending the night here very pleasantly, indulging in various luxuries such as a good varied dinner (greater in variety though more limited in certain things than our mess), eaten slowly, with a bit of wine, and music, a cigar afterwards, and a sense of quiet and freedom.

You need have no worry at all, for I am absolutely primed in every way, health, spirits, training, equipment. Hereafter I hope to be able to have more interesting things to write about to add to that epistolary classic which you have collected.

Much love to all.

On the Western Front

18th Squadron, R. F. C.
March 1st, France (1918)

Dear Mother and Father

Well, my guess which I made early in January about when I would get out here came true, for it was just after midnight last night when I came in. We had a very pleasant crossing, a beautiful day, almost a Hilltop day, warm and clear. We travelled up to a certain sort of distribution station from which the various squadrons draw. There one often has to wait a week or two, but I was lucky enough to get out the same evening, though I am sorry to say the two fellows I came with are left there. But they may come here later.

I was astonished at the smooth way that transportation was managed. At each stage our names were on a list and we were told at once what to do and where to go. The last stage of my journey, about forty miles, was made in a motor. It was quite fun tearing along through little dark towns, one after another, and over the countryside on the Lombardy-poplar-lined roads. It was an exquisite night, nearly full moon and not a cloud.

This squadron has more than come up to my hopes, the officers impress me as being nice chaps and I expect will be very pleasant to work with. I have noticed, while coming over and since being here, that as individuals the officers are much better than those we came across when in the training squadrons.

They seem more like real men doing a man's work, and it makes one feel a bit more of a man to be with them. I don't expect I shall do anything for a few days till I have a flip round the country and get used to my machine. I'll write at greater length then.

Hereafter you can use the above address and letters will come direct.   Much love.

18th Squadron, R. F. C.

B. E. F., France, March 2 (1918).

Dear Os,—

I have received a couple of letters from you written round Christmas time, but have waited to write you till I got out here and had something worth telling about. You know what a fuss the women make as soon as you get into a uniform. They begin attributing all sorts of brave qualities to you while you are safely training that you really scarcely deserve when actually in service, and it makes you feel a bit of an impostor till you are in a position where there is some ground for their implications. Then one feels better about it.

We are located well back of the lines where it is peaceful and quiet, only the big guns can be heard and they are just a sound, not a noise, just a reminder that there is a war on, which one often forgets in the fuss and stir that is often made over inconsequential things in training. But we work on a fairly important sector of the front and it is going to be vastly interesting. Our work is photography, reconnoissance and bombing, and it is therefore something different each trip and far more interesting than scout fighting or artillery ranging.

We have splendid machines, faster than anything in the air at high altitudes, and in a few months expect to have even better ones, an improvement on these. The casualties in our work are surprisingly few and yet our squadron has a good record for accounting for Huns that try to interrupt us. We only fight defensively, but are well able to do that. They give new men three weeks to get used to the machine and become familiar with the country before going over the lines. A very good way to work into it gradually, you see.

We live very comfortably in huts made of galvanized iron in the shape of a half-barrel cut lengthwise, with windows in the ends. They are divided into four rooms with just two officers in each, and so are roomy, secluded and comfortable. So far as possible a pilot rooms with his observer, for it is essential that they know each other well so as to have confidence in each other in the air and know what the other will do or would have you do in certain situations when it has to be done too quickly to give time for explanation, a little dual teamwork, and of course the better you work together, the better results you will achieve. We have a batman (orderly) to each hut, who keeps our boots, belts and buttons polished, a fire going in the morning and generally cleans up round, and when you go anywhere, packs up for you. Pretty soft! The mess is not a bit bad, and the officers in our squadron very pleasant chaps and they have been most agreeable to me on just coming in.

Three months from now I can begin to look for a couple of weeks' leave. Perhaps by that time you will be over and can get away for a day or two so we can meet and have a chat. I certainly hope so as I will be keen to see you and some of my friends I hope to get in contact with who are in various American camps over here. Pol Roger is only fifteen *francs* per quart, so we can have a good party. Here's to it! Cheery oh!

18th Squadron, R. F. C.
B. E. F., France, March 3 (1918)

Dear Beth,—

Just a line or two today, for I gave most of the news of my situation to Oswald in the letter I sent him by you.

Thus far the weather has been dull for flying, so I have been getting a good rest and have amused myself in reading and catching up with my correspondence. We have a fairly passable piano in the mess, so I am getting my hand in once more. When I left I forgot my music, which I left on your piano. Do you suppose you could gather it together and roll it up and send it to me? Have the ends open and label it, and it will come all right. There isn't much,—the four books of MacDowell, the old favourites, and one or two others. And if you happen to have anything that is interesting and not too hard I would enjoy working on it.

Unless the front line should change decidedly we are likely to remain here indefinitely, so I am getting settled down comfortably, arranging my things as I wish and putting little conveniences about here and there which give a touch of comfort and hominess to my billet. And on dull days I expect I can get quite a bit of time at the piano. I am very glad of that, for I have missed it greatly heretofore.

Speaking of dull days, when there is no flying we don't have to get up in the morning till we wish—up till 9.30, when break-fast is over; so our batman comes round to light the fire, and when we ask him what sort of a day it is, he replies, "Very prop-erly dull, sir." It is really a most leisurely life even on good days, for the work is only a matter of a few hours and then there is the rest and quiet of this camp. But it doesn't chafe one to do nothing out here as it did while in training, for we are on the spot and ready to work when weather permits. Other times all sorts of games of Rugby and field hockey are got up among ourselves or with the mechanics.

I went to a boxing match yesterday held at another camp and saw some very good boxing. But what was particularly amus-ing—I had no sooner entered the building than the band began to play the William Tell storm scene, and I almost imagined I was back in our library with the old Victrola.

I wish I could tell you where I am, for you could imagine when reading the *communiqués* whether I was in it or not, but it is absolutely forbidden. Also cameras are not permitted in France in the army, so I can take no pictures. I am sorry about that, for they would make an interesting record, but I will have to make increased effort to draw the pictures in words.

18th Squadron, R. F. C.
B. E. F., France, March 4, 1918.

Dear Father and Mother,—

The weather has continued bad for flying, so I have been free to get settled down here. Unlike in training, one doesn't mind bad weather with its delays, for we aren't set at arbitrary work for the mere sake of being busy, but can use the time as we wish. Also it used to be unpleasant to have anything delay my com-ing out here, but once here it doesn't matter, for we are on the spot and ready, and if we can't fly, neither can the Hun, so such a wait isn't a waste of time.

I am getting better acquainted with the fellows now and they have included me in their number very pleasantly. I was partic-ularly gratified that the observer I am rooming with asked es-pecially to be detailed to work with me, for he had only myself to judge by, not having seen me fly yet. It is most fortunate for me, as he has had several months' experience in the work and knows the country well. He is a Scotchman, fine-looking and most agreeable, about twenty-eight or thirty, I should judge, with lots of common sense and poise. I can feel complete confidence in him when I go up, and you can readily see that is important to successful co-operation in emergencies. He was a bombing officer in the infantry before joining the R. F. C. and has been in since the beginning, having fought in France, Egypt and Salonika, and is most interesting to talk to. I shall be well off working with him, so you need have less anxiety. Living together this way we often get talking of our work, and he can give me many valuable points and tips.

We live in a cosy little hut and I am getting it all fixed up with the little conveniences which make for one's comfort. I dare say we shall be here perhaps permanently so long as I am in France, so I can completely unpack and feel at home. I am going to tack up the various pictures which I have of you all, and of my friends, and so I will seem actually with you all the time. We have a new piano in the mess and several fairly good players, and I shall get a lot of pleasure out of it, for I can take myself completely out of my surroundings when playing, and find lots of calm comfort in it.

We have plenty of the things that are short elsewhere in our mess,—that is, sugar, butter, bread, etc., and nice jam for breakfast and tea,—so if you are sending me the periodical food-boxes you needn't include any sugar, and I find I can buy dates in the near-by town very reasonably, but they haven't good figs. So what you might send now is figs, chocolate, fruit-cake,—I haven't had a bit of cake for months and I understand fruit-cake keeps well,—Lord Salisbury cigarettes and matches. You might put in a ten-cent tin of Lucky Strike tobacco also, for French tobacco is quite impossible and I don't like English. These things will come through out here all right if you send them to the address above, and I believe you have to leave an end so it can be opened.

Don't try to send much at once, just a small parcel which can come quickly by mail, and it will be such a treat to receive it. Put in three or four boxes of matches, for they are extremely scarce, and tell Oswald to bring some with him for himself when he comes. He needn't bother about sugar except a little to use when on leave, for they seem to keep the army well supplied. Everyone carries a little bottle of saccharine when he goes out to tea in England and it works very well. I should appreciate a book from time to time, as we do a good deal of reading on off days. But you don't need to feel any sympathy, for we are unpardonably comfortable. I think if you would send me *Current Opinion* it would be nice, as it deals with much in addition to the war and gives good summaries. I believe it comes out once a month or fortnight. I seem to be asking for a good deal, but I expect you want to do things, and these I would appreciate greatly.

Much love to all the family.

To His Younger Brother

18th Squadron, R. F. C.

B. E. F., France, March 4, 1918.

Dear Linc,—

I have been meaning to write you for a long time, but I am carrying a rather large correspondence with the various spread-out members of the family; so I decided to let yours go until I got out here, believing you would be pleased to know I am actually in active service at the Front, at last. Father enclosed one of your letters to him, written in January, and I am glad to hear from it that you are getting along so well in track. But a recent letter from Mother, telling me of her visit to Mr. Meigs, and your results since, have pleased me more; for you seem, at last, to be playing the game, and that is the right thing for you to do. If you can make good at Hill in *studies*, as well as socially and in athletics, then you will have acquired the habits of mind and morals to insure your success in anything else you may undertake—war or business.

But you must remember to be cautious, and not be content, or relax after one week of good record; it means day after day, month after month, never relaxing your pace, to get anywhere near the top. The man who is at the top has no better equipment than you have, but merely used what he had to the utmost; and you must learn that there is absolutely nothing you cannot do if you set your mind to it. It is a case of ambition and desire sufficiently strong to make untiring effort worth while.

In this flying game, for instance, I have felt that my individual excellence would do much toward insuring my return. There, you see, was the desire—life or death—as incentive to make my utmost effort to master all my work.

As a result, I am glad to tell you that I went through the gunnery school in Scotland with an average mark of 94%, which was the best of my group of twenty fellows; in other words, mental as well as physical superiority. Yet I was not so well equipped as some. I didn't waste my time, or let myself be content with "well-enough," but only with the best.

You may see no value or connection in your doing likewise in the matter of Latin verbs, and such things; but there is a connection; for it is not the verb which you master, it is the dent in your brain which the effort to master has put there, and it will make the next job you tackle that much easier for you to do.

When so much besides your own welfare depends upon your playing the game to the limit,—the ease of mind and gratification it will mean to Mother and Father; the increased freedom which I can feel to meet whatever may come to me, knowing that my absence, if I should fall, will be no permanent loss, and that you are learning to live so that you can fill my place in the Adams line; I am sure you will do your best.

Also, when you flunk a job, you are not getting out of it the value equivalent to the money which Father puts in. That is a waste, and even that waste, indirect as it may seem, does affect the total, and so is wrong in times like these. I am confident you will do the right thing, but you must remember that a succession of spurts will never win the race. That just wears you out. It is the steady pace, which all the time grows a little stronger, that pulls you out ahead. Stick to it!

I haven't much war news to give you yet, for I have only been out here at the Front a few days, and the weather has been too bad to fly. But we are in a most interesting section of the Front, near a place you have often read about, and all the time we can hear the sound of the big guns, which occasionally increases to steady thunder when Fritz starts a raid, or something. It will be lively here this summer, and I shall have some interesting stories to tell you when I get home.

Active Service

18th Squadron, R. F. C.
B. E. F., France, March 7, 1918.

Dear Mother and Father,—

I have now added the last few touches to my room and it is indeed cosy. On the walls round about my table I have tacked up pictures of all the family and some of my friends, "Poof," "Woof," Elmer, etc., and sitting here in the seclusion with your faces all about me I am very happy. I even have the picture of our house which was on the calendar. And when it rains the patter of the drops on the galvanized iron roof muffled by the sheathing inside carries me way back to the old Irvingcroft house with its tin roofs. Such is the association of ideas, for I no sooner heard it than the old house came into my mind.

But there is such a lot of comfort in pictures,—I never realised it so truly before. I look at one and seem to talk to it on the view of interest with that one, thus with the next, and I switch onto that bond. Even old Grandpa Kilburn is here, and of course all the kids, though I haven't a good picture of "Howie." How you all seem to be looking at me so nicely, and how I love you all for the kind wishes and love I see in your eyes.

The last two days have been wonderfully clear and warm, so our squadron has pulled off a couple of "shows." Perhaps if I describe one so far as I saw it, and as what I didn't see was reported to me, it will give you a little better idea of the procedure.

Every morning our batman reports on the weather prospects, and when it is clear we have to get up a bit earlier. After breakfast a conference is held at which the purpose and objective of the trip are given and any details arranged for. Then the men who are going put on their flying kit and go out to the machines. These have previously been rolled out of the hangars, filled up with fuel, guns loaded, bombs, cameras, etc., attached, and everything shipshape. Each pilot gets in, the engine is started and warmed up, finally the chocks are pulled away from the wheels and the machines taxi out onto the aerodrome and line up ready to take off, the engine snorting and sputtering impatiently.

As they wobble over the ground the machines look so clumsy and ill at ease, with tails dragging and bumping, noses up in the air. The leader takes his place on the line, his machine indicated by some streamers. There have been no farewells or good-luck wishes, the men have started off as if they were off in a car to go to an office; it is not masked indifference, it is simple matter of course.

All are ready, and the leader, followed immediately by the others, opens out the throttle, and the machines move faster and faster, tails up now and noses low and level, like a runner stooping a bit on his run before a spring. The wheels trip along, each time touching more lightly, till with a final bound the machine is clear. What a fearful roar they make, great powerful engines unmuffled, wide open.

One after another they leap into the air and at once are transformed from ugly ducklings to beautiful swans, at home and happy in their natural element, as they arch round and round, ever higher. Finally when they are sufficiently high they move off in their close formation in an arrow line for their objective, finally fading out of sight.

Some hours later they come in sight again and glide in, some as fresh as when they left, others so badly cut up you wonder how the machine could hold together. Then we hear the story told in the form of a simple report, still all as a matter of course. How they flew undisturbed to their objective though noticing a large number of Huns in various parts of the sky as they flew along. But when they turned to come back the Huns had gathered over thirty counted against our four, a veritable swarm between them and home.

And yet without hesitation our machines fly straight at them! They break up into groups and surround our machines on all sides, above, below, each side, before, behind, all discharging their venomous sting when a good sight is obtained, darting in for a burst of shots, soaring up or diving away one after another, a continuous *mêlée*. Our machines zigzag from time to time, but always progress toward home unless some Hun more persistent than others has to be turned on.

Meanwhile our men, scarcely knowing which machine to pick out to fire at, keep sending off bursts whenever they get a good sight. When a Hun receives a burst a bit too close he dives for home, and when a machine is hit, several others accompany it down for a way to cool off. They are no sports, these Huns, they will never attack unless with overwhelming odds, and even then they never come across the lines, so in case of engine failure they are sure to get safely home. Yet our few machines over hostile territory fly straight into the swarm of them, bring down six, and all return and have but one man hit. It isn't luck that they come through; it is superior shooting due to a large steady machine, a sporting blood in the men that makes them play the game, no matter what the odds.

Though the Hun has a decided advantage fighting over his own territory, it is a large factor in his defeat, for it is an open acknowledgment of his inferiority, and it only takes a little spirit and some cool shooting to make him sick. You see, Mother, no matter what the odds, we have all the advantage, and, after all, it is seldom that they get as large a bunch as that together. For instance, on the "show" today not a single one was sighted. So at their worst you see you have little to worry about, and they are seldom at their worst. Also we never fight except defensively, only when they interfere with our work or try to keep us from getting home, and then they regret it, for we are well equipped for defence.

I wouldn't have given all these details if I were not sure you would extract the interest and not let the exciting features make you worry. For I want you to know all about the work and yet see in it the small element of danger and the very great interest which you couldn't have if I told nothing about it for fear of worrying you. There are some Hun machines which will go higher than these we use, but there is no machine made by any nation as fast at the high altitude where we work; and speed is king.

Must get to bed now. Much love to all.

March 11 (1918).

Dear Father and Mother,—

Two days ago another batch of letters came, including a couple of papers and the little album which I was most amused to look over. The valentine from Mother was much appreciated, with its nice sentiment. By the way, so far as possible it would be a good idea for you all to let Father put your letters in his envelopes with his official stamp on them, for they always seem to get here several days before the others when written at the same time. I believe they go through the censor in England more quickly. There was a nice letter from Grace in the bunch and Mother's of the 10th. Also a very nice long letter from Mrs. Cameron, Woof's mother, whom I wrote in January for Woof's address. She was awfully good to us while at college, and I spent many happy week-ends out at their home in Westford.

I have sent several pictures cut from papers to Grace showing various phases of our work, and if they get through to her, as no doubt they will, she will send them to you. If she doesn't want them back will you keep them for me, as we aren't allowed to have cameras in France, and I will want them as a record for my scrapbook when I return.

You must expect mails to take longer from out here and to be more irregular, but I hope you will not allow yourselves to become alarmed if a long period elapses at any time, for if there were any cause due to me, you would have heard long before the gap came by cable. And now don't hold your breath in apprehension of a cable any day. Contrary to your belief, Mother, I am in one of the very safest branches I could be in because of our splendid machines which are faster than anything in the air at the altitudes where we work—over three miles up.

And in a very few months we are to have even better machines, the same as these, only improved. Our work is safer than that of the others because of the machines, the height, and the fact that we don't look for trouble, but only fight when attacked; and on Wednesday last, when Haig congratulated the brigade for bringing down eighteen Huns, our one squadron, perfectly peaceable by nature, taught six out of that number that we can well defend ourselves. On that occasion, over thirty Huns attacked only four of ours, and ours all came back.

But while we are on the subject I want to caution you about a possibility. One of our machines has been reported missing a day or so ago, but it was only engine failure and the machine was seen to have safely landed, so the occupants are safe but unhappily detained in Hun-land. Frequently no word is brought from them, and no one sees what became of a machine. So you see, a man may be quite all right who simply disappeared and was reported missing. The case is not likely to arise, however, as our engines as a rule are very reliable. It is merely a possibility which in case it happened I want you to know there is no need to worry—less than ever, for it would mean simply a safe but long wait for the war to end.

I think I am receiving all your mail, as there have not been any wide gaps in their dates; the gaps come only in their receipt. Four of Grace's were lost, but they were among the earlier ones; we write several times a week usually, so we know if any are lost. Possibly some may have been on the cruiser that was lost last week; if so, I shall know in a short while. But I believe the mail is distributed among a number of ships as a rule, so only a small amount is lost with one ship. That ship, by the way, convoyed us over, so I am familiar with her.

The new uniform I had made in London when I left came today and is very good-looking. It will be nice to have to change into for dinner, and for going on leave, etc. I am getting all the time more comfortably settled and am very happy here. Each day I manage to get in a flight of an hour or two, becoming familiar with the country, meanwhile picking up many valuable points from talking with the fellows.

Love to all.

(Received on Easter Morning—1918)

Mother Mine,—

This is just a little Easter greeting to make you know I am actually close by you all the time. May it give you much cheer and happiness.

Tender love.

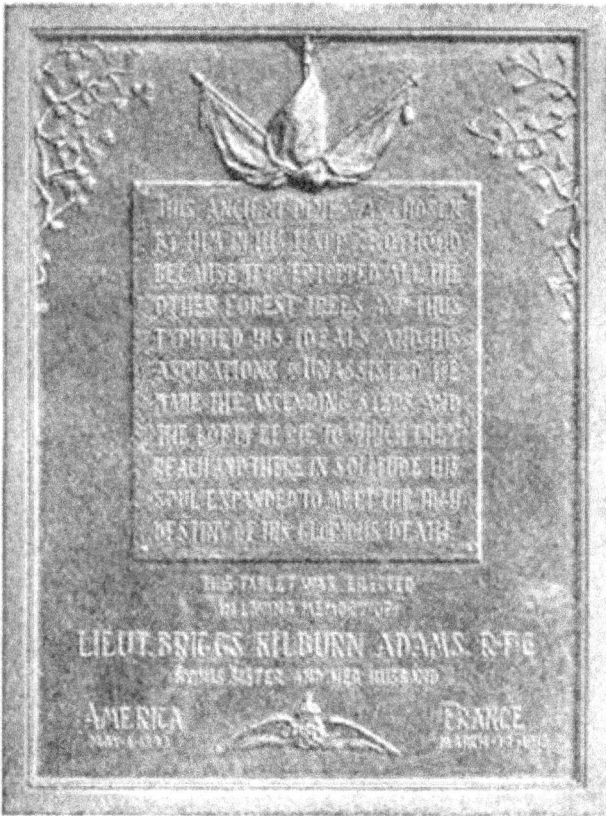

MEMORIAL TABLET ERECTED BY LIEUTENANT ADAMS'S SISTER AND HER
HUSBAND, CAPTAIN O. D. PFOELZER, ON AN OLD PINE TREE IN THE
FOREST AT HILLTOP FARMS, LITTLETON, NEW HAMPSHIRE.